ADVANCE PRAISE

"Dale has given us a how-to guide on becoming a modern auto retailer. Every dealer should hold a series of managers meetings to strategically address the issues raised in the book. *Like I See It* is an insurance policy for every dealer's financial future."

—Mark Rikess, president, The Rikess Group

"This book is a must read for those that want to prepare for, and profit from, the automotive disruption that is ahead."

—Brian Benstock, vice president,
Paragon Honda and Paragon Acura

"If you're a student of the car business, you should put Dale Pollak's *Like I See It* on the office shelf, right next to his *Velocity* books. If you're not drinking his Kool-Aid now, you will be soon."

—Mike Shaw, president and owner, Mike Shaw Automotive

"The auto industry is fortunate to have a thinker like Dale amongst us. With *Like I See It*, he uses his enlightened common sense and unconventional thinking to point out opportunities for dealers to improve their businesses today. Dale has a way of knowing what's around the next bend before the rest of us do, and this book provides a glimpse of the future that is both exciting and frightening."

—Alan Haig, founder, Haig Partners

"Being a dealer has never been more challenging. Dale speaks to that reality and not only confronts the uncomfortable truths but also does the more important work of providing solutions. As a dealer advocate, Dale's a precious and valuable resource."

—**Steve Germain,** president, The Germain Auto Group

"Dale Pollak is uniquely qualified to address the pressing issues in auto retail. His provocative presentation takes on the difficult environment dealers face with real-world solutions that combine technology, process, and drastic policy change. Dale quickly turns readers into 'raving fans' who appreciate his deep retail experience and ability to use technology to move a dealer's focus from art to science."

—**Mike Maroone,** CEO, Mike Maroone Automotive and former president and COO, AutoNation

LIKE
I SEE IT

LIKE
I SEE IT

**OBSTACLES AND OPPORTUNITIES SHAPING
THE FUTURE OF RETAIL AUTOMOTIVE**

DALE POLLAK

vAuto Press

Published by vAuto Press
Oakbrook Terrace, IL
www.vauto.com

Copyright ©2017 vAuto, Inc.

All rights reserved.

Distributed by Greenleaf Book Group

For ordering information or special discounts for bulk purchases, please contact Greenleaf Book Group at PO Box 91869, Austin, TX 78709, 512.891.6100.

Design and composition by Greenleaf Book Group
Cover design by The Mx Group, www.themxgroup.com
Photo of Dale with Pope Francis courtesy of the author

Cataloging-in-Publication data is available.

Print ISBN: 978-0-9992427-0-4

eBook ISBN: 978-0-9992427-1-1

Part of the Tree Neutral® program, which offsets the number of trees consumed in the production and printing of this book by taking proactive steps, such as planting trees in direct proportion to the number of trees used: www.treeneutral.com

Printed in the United States of America on acid-free paper

18 19 20 21 22 23   10 9 8 7 6 5 4 3 2

First Edition

CONTENTS

ACKNOWLEDGMENTS

I must first acknowledge and thank my colleagues and friends at Cox Enterprises and Cox Automotive for giving me the encouragement, opportunity, and support to write this book. In particular, I am ever grateful to executive leaders John Dyer, outgoing president and CEO of Cox Enterprises; Alex Taylor, incoming president and CEO of Cox Enterprises; and Sandy Schwartz, president of Cox Automotive, for their ongoing friendship, respect, and trust. This book is really an extension of our collective Cox commitment to ensure the ongoing success and vibrancy of franchise and independent dealers and their partners, without whom there would be no retail automotive industry.

I am indebted to a long list of dealers and others in our industry for sharing your insights and perspectives. You've corrected me when I veered off course, kept me honest, and provided untold assistance as this book has come to life. There are too many of you to name; but you know who you are.

I must also thank the entire vAuto team for their tireless commitment and loyalty to our dealer clients and the business. I view vAuto much like a parent views a child who has gone on to success in life. You can't ever fully let go, and it's a beautiful thing to see the success carry on, day in and day out.

I also need to thank two individuals, who effectively serve as my right and left hands, respectively.

The first is my executive assistant, Susan Taft, who ensures I get to where I need to be and meet the people I need to meet, every day. I am able to do the things I do because Susan is always there to cover my back and anticipate any obstacle I might not see.

The second is Lance Helgeson, who once again served as my eyes, ears, and wordsmith as I undertook another book-writing project. Lance's can-do spirit and ability to strike the just-right perspective and tone in words continue to be a benefit and blessing for me.

Of course, this book would not be possible without the generosity, love, patience, support, and understanding of my family. More and more, I realize that without them, there would be no me. I consider my wife, Nancy, as the rock that helps me roll. And each of my sons, Austin, Alex, and Samson, stands behind and beside me like a stalwart spirit soldier. Sometimes it seems like they know and understand me better than I do—which may be the ultimate gift any husband and father can hope for.

Finally, I must acknowledge you, the reader. Chances are better than good you didn't pick up this book by mistake. You've come to these pages with a purpose. I view your interest and trust in my perspective as a precious gift that I hold dear.

INTRODUCTION

I hadn't planned to write this book.

I've been extremely fortunate that my three previous books, which addressed the Velocity Method of Management, have been so well received by dealers and the retail automotive industry as a whole.

I felt like the books made a real difference. They introduced Velocity principles and fostered a new way of thinking about the used car business. Thousands of dealers took the principles to heart and applied them in their businesses.

For most dealers, the Velocity journey wasn't easy. They butted heads with managers who resisted new ways of doing business. They took significant financial lumps. They sometimes had to let go of longtime, loyal employees.

But the same dealers would tell you the Velocity-based aggravation, extra effort, and pain was worth it. Many are selling more used cars and making more money from their dealerships than they considered possible. They understand that they've adopted a more resilient, sustainable model for retailing used vehicles that meets today's era of market efficiency and transparency.

The success the dealers achieved gave me satisfaction. I felt like the Velocity books accomplished my goal of giving something meaningful back to a business that has given me, and my family, so many blessings over the years. I was proud of the books, and, at some level, I thought they represented all I might say about the car business.

But since my last book, I've had a growing sense that the car business, and dealers, might be in more trouble than anyone cares to understand, or even consider.

I've come to believe that our industry is at a critical turning point in its evolution, thanks to the ever-faster confluence of technology and changing consumer preferences.

As I've traveled the country, and paid attention to the everyday struggles of dealers, I've begun to realize that the future prosperity of our industry is by no means secure.

I've seen little evidence that dealers, original equipment manufacturers (OEM), and solution providers understand how much the way they conduct business today is harmful to themselves, and each other, and diminishes the potential of our industry for future generations. It's been frustrating to feel, time and again, that I'm apparently the only guy in the room who's willing to call out these industry elephants for what they really are—an impediment for everyone.

At the most fundamental level, our industry remains plagued by a legacy of inefficiency and lack of transparency. The persistent harm of this legacy owes to two factors.

1. THE SEMI-SYMBIOTIC NATURE OF OUR INDUSTRY

In the car business, everyone's fortunes are tightly tied together. Each stakeholder group—factories, dealers, and solution providers—affects the other. When one group suffers, the others typically feel it. You'd think this environment would foster more collaboration and cooperation.

Unfortunately, the outcome is exactly the opposite. Everyone looks out mostly for themselves, creating a prime breeding ground for the inaction, inattention, and ill-fated decisions that allow inefficiency and lack of transparency to linger on. I fear these factors are slowly eroding the common bond that, in the past, served to unite dealers in the face of shared adversity.

2. THE CURSE OF SUCCESS

Irish playwright George Bernard Shaw is credited with saying, "Success covers a multitude of blunders." This is an apt description for the car business, which has enjoyed an extremely good run the past several years. Everyone's making good money. But amid these good times, no one seems to be paying much attention to the ways that inefficiency and lack of transparency sap the industry's true potential today and tomorrow.

Well, I have been paying attention, and the time has come to speak up.

Consider this book as one man's attempt to help dealers, OEMs, and solution providers get smart—to start thinking about the ways that inefficiency and lack of transparency remain a persistent problem at all levels of the industry and to offer a more collectively minded approach that will help everyone build a better, more profitable, and prosperous retail automotive industry for tomorrow.

This book isn't about Velocity principles. The focus here is much broader, with chapters intended to address specific areas of inefficiency and lack of transparency that pose the biggest obstacles and opportunities for all of us.

By no means is this book intended to be an end-all, be-all guide for the future. The car business is evolving too quickly for anyone to offer a prescriptive plan for the way forward.

But it is my sincere hope, however, that this book spurs much-needed conversations and helps set guideposts that help dealers, OEMs, and solution providers improve the way they do business for themselves and each other.

Just as my previous books ruffled some feathers across the industry, I expect this one will do the same. My apologies in advance to those who might take affront or offense. Simply put, I'd be doing myself and everyone else a disservice if I didn't stay true to my nature, and my bond to other dealers, and call it like I see it.

Thank you for your interest. Enjoy the read.

1

MARGIN COMPRESSION: WHY SIMPLY SELLING MORE CARS WON'T BE ENOUGH

E ver since the dawn of the franchise dealer, there's been a fairly simple formula for success. Each year, dealers would aim to do better than they did the year before. If they could, they'd find ways to increase the gross profit they earned for every new and used retail unit. If they couldn't make more on a per-car basis, they'd focus on growing their retail volumes to produce a higher level of gross profit than they achieved in the prior year.

It's fair to say this sell-more-to-make-more formula has served the car business very well over the past hundred years.

But I believe the formula is quickly running out of gas—and its demise means bad news for nearly every dealer in the country.

The chief culprit is margin compression.

Thanks to the Internet, rising transparency, and a highly competitive market, dealers aren't making as much money on a per-car basis as they used to. What's more, we're not too far away from a normalization of new and used vehicle sales volumes, where the year-over-year increases dealers have enjoyed since 2009 will at least flatline, if not decline.

For dealers, these converging trends will render the old formula for success—that you can make up declines in front-end grosses by selling more cars—highly problematic.

Let's take a moment to unpack and validate these trends.

In 2005, dealers had a stellar year. According to stats from the National Automobile Dealers Association (NADA), dealers averaged 852 new vehicle sales per rooftop, contributing to an annual total of 16.9 million new retail units. Profits were pretty good, too. New vehicle gross profit as a percentage of transaction prices ran roughly 5 percent. With an average vehicle transaction price of $28,400, the front-end gross profit average ran $1,420.

Of course, the bottom had fallen out of the industry by 2009. Thanks to the economic recession, new vehicle sales dropped to 10.4 million that year (down 39 percent from their 2005 peak). The average dealership retailed 615 new vehicles. Even worse, the gross profits on those vehicles also went south.

NADA data shows that gross profit as a percentage of transaction prices ran 3.61 percent in 2009. With an average transaction price of $28,966, the average front-end gross profit for dealers that year ran $1,045—a 26 percent decline from the tally in 2005.

Since that time, the industry has gained considerable steam.

In 2011, NADA reported that dealers saw a positive profit in their new vehicle departments for the first time in five years—an achievement that largely owes to the pent-up demand for new cars after the recession.

This blessing of strong demand for new vehicles has only continued.

I vividly remember the mood at NADA's 2014 convention in New Orleans. Dealers had just closed their fourth consecutive year of collectively selling over one million more new vehicles than they had the year before. "Business is fantastic!" was a common refrain. Even NADA's convention theme, "Accelerate Your Business," seemed spot-on.

Sure enough, dealers closed 2014 selling 16.4 million new vehicles, with the average dealership selling 1,003 units for the year. Gross margins, however, didn't fare so well.

NADA reports the front-end gross profit as a percentage of vehicle transaction price in 2014 ran 2.48 percent—which translates to $808 per car, given a $32,618 average transaction price.

By my calculations, these figures mean that dealers saw a 43 percent decline in front-end gross profits in new vehicles between 2005 and 2014. Over the course of the same period, dealers paid 20 percent more on average to purchase this inventory from their factory partners, according to Kelley Blue Book data on invoice prices.

> "No matter how you slice it, dealers are investing more to acquire the vehicles they sell, and seeing a smaller return when they retail the vehicles and recoup their investment."

I wish I could report that margin compression has only affected new vehicles through the past decade. Unfortunately, it's wreaking a bit of havoc in used vehicles, too.

In 2005, the average used vehicle transaction price was $14,925, according to NADA. At that time, the front-end gross profit as a percentage of transaction prices ran roughly 12 percent, or $1,791 per unit.

But in 2014, dealers saw an average used vehicle transaction price of roughly $18,700. Meanwhile, the front-end gross profit as a percentage of transaction prices ran 8.6 percent, or $1,608 per unit—a 10 percent decline from 2005.

No matter how you slice it, dealers are investing more to acquire the vehicles they sell, and seeing a smaller return when they retail the vehicles and recoup their investment. This profit-draining trend in new and used vehicles will only get worse.

Why, then, aren't dealers all that concerned?

When I ask dealers about these effects of margin compression, I'll often hear comments like this one:

"Our grosses are about the same as they've always been. Sure, we might be able to do better, but we're selling more cars, new and used. We're having a record year. I don't really see margin compression as a problem."

I understand the source of these sentiments. This dealer, like many of his peers, is banking on the industry's age-old formula for success—if you sell more cars, you'll make your profit through volume.

But I question whether, in today's ever-present era of declining margins, this formula will work for the long haul.

Consider these five factors that are likely to further erode profits for many dealers.

1. Volume limits

Ours is a highly cyclical business. Old car dogs like me can't help but worry that the next downturn is right around the corner. Maybe we'll get lucky. Maybe the industry won't take a big hit due to some kind of shock, economic or otherwise. Maybe it'll be as some analysts predict. We'll see another year or two of incremental growth in new vehicle sales and might even surpass the eighteen million vehicle mark. After that, sales will level off and likely diminish. The key question, though, is how far will volumes fall, and what will the decline mean for dealers who depend on the age-old formula for their profitability and success?

I'm afraid the outlook for these dealers won't be so good. There simply won't be the opportunity to sell as many new vehicles as they're retailing today. Plus there's no assurance that factories will continue to help offset front-end margin declines through stair-step bonus money. In my view, it's not a question of if these factors converge but how soon it'll happen. When it does, margin compression will no longer be an abstract concept; it'll be a very real and serious problem.

2. Interest expense

When I was a dealer in the 1980s, interest expense was a much bigger deal than it is today. We routinely paid interest rates above 10 percent when we borrowed money for facilities or floorplan. Today, dealers pay a fraction of yesteryear's interest expense, and they aren't complaining.

But while I don't believe we'll see double-digit interest rates, there's only one direction they can move from their historically low levels, which is up.

As the Fed makes these adjustments, many dealers risk being overexposed in two key areas.

The first is floorplan expense. In recent years, top-performing dealers have turned factory floorplan programs into moneymakers. With ultralow interest rates, and a focus on inventory velocity, these dealers have turned an expense into a profit driver. Even less investment-efficient dealers do OK. For them, floorplan expense is a break-even proposition, as they use faster-selling units to pay down the interest costs of slower-moving inventory.

The bottom line: Floorplan expense hasn't burdened the balance sheet much in recent years—an operational benefit that will diminish in direct proportion to the size of any interest rate increase.

The second risk area relates to the interest on loans dealers use to finance facilities and real estate. Being the gamblers they are, it's not uncommon for dealers to take out floating, rather than fixed, rate loans. It's been a good gamble in light of historically low rates. But the prospect of an interest rate increase has spurred astute, forward-thinking dealers to fix these arrangements to minimize future exposure.

3. F&I regulation

As front-end profits decline in new and used vehicles, dealers have leaned on their F&I offices to help them achieve the level of profitability they expect from their variable operations. In 2005, F&I revenue accounted for about 25 percent of gross profit generated in variable operations. In 2016, the figure ran north of 40 percent, and it's still climbing.

That's really good money.

But, looking ahead, I suspect it'll be difficult for dealers to expect a similar trajectory of increased profit production from F&I, particularly as federal agencies, like the Consumer Finance Protection Bureau (CFPB), put heat on lenders to limit dealer reserve markups and question the sales practices and transparency of F&I products.

At the moment, NADA is working to limit CFPB's authority and oversight of F&I practices.

But even if NADA succeeds, it seems to me the die is cast. I wouldn't be surprised if the terms of American Honda's settlement agreement with CFPB don't become more or less standard practice for the industry—a development that will affect every dealer and cause those who over-rely on F&I income the highest level of profitability pain.

4. Competition

In my work to advance Velocity Method of Management principles in new and used vehicle operations at dealerships, I've discovered you can divide dealers into three groups. The top performers account for about 10 percent of all dealers. They are progressive. They keep a close eye on future trends. They have a clear view of how much margin compression has affected their performance and profitability. Some have already begun to actively combat margin compression across their dealerships.

The next group makes up another 10 to 20 percent of dealers. They don't lead the pack, but they adapt to change more quickly than most. They, too, recognize margin compression as a risk but aren't necessarily sure how best to address it.

The third group, the remaining 70 percent, are more reactive to market trends. They like proof before they proceed. It often takes a crisis to spur them to action. They're like the dealer who doesn't view margin compression as an imminent threat.

As sales volumes diminish, and margin compression becomes

more profound, the dealers in the top 10 percent are going to have a field day. Their efforts to curtail margin compression today will give them a competitive advantage when the market becomes more challenging tomorrow. They're the ones buying up the competition and using ever-larger economies and efficiencies of scale to their distinct advantage (more on this in chapter 13).

The success of these dealers will largely come at the expense of dealers in the third group. Unfortunately, they will work harder and harder, applying the age-old "sell more, make more" formula and hoping for success that just doesn't seem to materialize. Over time, they will see, in painfully clear terms, how far this fractured formula falls short as viable retail strategy in today's retail environment.

5. Ongoing margin compression

As noted previously, you can trace the root causes of margin compression in automotive retail to the Internet. Consumers now have unprecedented levels of efficiency and transparency as they look to buy, sell, and service vehicles. By their nature, these market dynamics are disruptive to dealer margins.

But the same is true in every other retail sector. The Internet has made it harder for virtually every retailer to make more money. Those who do find the gains flow through increased efficiencies, not just selling more stuff.

Dealers should not make the mistake of thinking that margin compression will somehow, someday, just go away. As with any business today, particularly one as mature as the automotive retail industry, margin compression is an ongoing fact and an increasingly troubling way of life.

AN EFFICIENCY- AND PROFIT-FOCUSED FORMULA

In light of all the evidence that margin compression is here to stay, and dealers won't always be able to count on year-over-year increases to remain profitable and prosperous, I suggest that dealers rethink the age-old, sell-more-and-make-more formula for success.

I'd rewrite the formula this way: You can make up the decline in front-end profit only if you sell more cars more *efficiently*.

This new formula is, in fact, the strategy that a growing number of top-performing dealers—the 10 percenters—have already begun to pursue at their dealerships.

These dealers recognize that while they can't necessarily stop margin compression, they can fight its harmful effects by changing *how* they do business. Their new way of doing business emphasizes technology-driven economic and operational efficiencies in all corners of the dealership. The dealers regard this strategy as the foundation for their future profitability and prosperity as retailers.

How does it look? Here are broad strokes that apply to four critical assets for every dealer.

Asset 1: Customers

Dealers have traditionally engaged customers on terms more favorable to the dealer than those they serve. You can't get beyond the asking price for a vehicle unless you come into the showroom. In the dealership, the sales process is built on long waits for customers that follows a "hold 'em 'til you fold 'em" strategy. In service, it's often left to customers to set appointments and to find out when their vehicle is ready and how much repairs will cost.

All of these inefficiencies can be eliminated through technology-driven processes that help dealers serve customers on the terms they prefer. The elimination of these inefficiencies would engender a higher level of customer loyalty and satisfaction. Dealers would benefit from improved productivity and profitability from their people (e.g., sales associates, managers, service advisors, even technicians), which yields a more positive financial outcome for the dealership.

Progressive dealers have already begun retooling their dealership people and processes to achieve a higher level of customer-centric efficiencies. In this way, they are fulfilling the promise of the new formula for success—profit improvement follows the elimination of long-standing inefficiencies.

Asset 2: Inventory

Currently, one of the most inefficient uses of dealer capital resides in new and used vehicle inventories. In 2016, the average

age of new vehicles in the majority of dealership inventories ran higher than one hundred days. By contrast, top-performing dealers achieve an average inventory age around seventy days—a benchmark that represents a 50 percent improvement in new vehicle inventory and sales velocity. These dealers have upended the traditional thinking that aging new vehicle inventory isn't a problem. They've adopted technology and tools to help them manage the complexity of inventory decisions—orders from the factory, dealer trades, add-on options, merchandising, pricing, and so on—in a manner that maximizes profitability and return on investment. These dealers have a clearer view of current market demands and optimize their inventory investments to meet them, even when factory allocations and restrictions make the job more difficult.

In used vehicles, dealers are doing a much better job than they have in years past. There's widespread recognition that aged vehicles are really symptoms of profit-draining inefficiencies. The best dealers retail 55 percent or more of their used vehicle inventories in less than thirty days. They understand that this more efficient and faster pace of inventory velocity translates to a higher level of profitability, sales, and total return on investment for the dealership itself. Still, there's room for improvement, particularly as the used vehicle market in the coming years will see increased supplies and a higher level of volatility.

Asset 3: People

As the industry has emerged from the 2007–2008 downturn, dealers have not been as efficiency minded or judicious as they have increased capacity and staff to meet growing market demand for new and used vehicles. Only a small minority of dealers tore up the traditional playbook and processes that inherently make people less efficient and productive in the showroom and beyond. Employee turnover in variable operations remains a costly, inefficient problem for dealers, even if

> **"Employee turnover in variable operations remains a costly, inefficient problem for dealers, even if these costs don't show up directly on dealership financial statements."**

these costs don't show up directly on dealership financial statements. I've devoted chapter 6 of this book to what I call *human capital management efficiency*. We'll dig deeper into the ways dealers can directly tie increased employee efficiency and productivity to profit improvement for the dealership. Suffice it to say, however, there's much, much work to be done.

Asset 4: Facilities

Dealers are in a bit of a bind when it comes to the high cost of facilities and land for their dealerships. Factory image programs remain a source of significant discontent. Factory-mandated costs to rebuild or renovate often don't pencil against the reality of margin compression and changing buyer needs and preferences. To be sure, dealers who diligently execute the efficiency-focused formula for success have an easier time saying yes when the factory requires additional investment. In upcoming chapters, we'll address a few considerations factories would do well to think about as they ask their dealers to make ever-higher investments and to perform continually better in a market that poses a higher level of future uncertainty than we've seen in recent years.

My hope is that this discussion of margin compression provides an eye-opening wake-up call for dealers. The time to take action is now—before the market turns and diminished profitability becomes an albatross that impedes your ability to achieve a profitable and prosperous future.

2

A QUIET KILLER OF THE CAR BUSINESS

As a former dealer, I fondly remember the days when the factory bonus checks arrived. $8,000. $15,000. $25,000.

It was the early 1990s, and Cadillac was among several manufacturers that rewarded dealers for meeting customer satisfaction and sales volumes targets.

We missed the mark a time or two, due more to market forces than any mistakes we made. In fact, we hit our targets with enough regularity that I felt confident I could count on the factory money.

I loved it. Back then, we made enough off our front-end gross profits to run the dealership and achieve the return on investment I expected from the business. The factory money was like gravy, and it arrived below the line. It wasn't part of the gross profit pool used to pay commissions, and it wasn't necessary for me to run my business.

Simply put, I could use the money as I saw fit. If I wanted to reinvest the money in the dealership, I could. If I wanted to spend it on something for my family or myself, I could do that, too.

My, oh my, how things have changed—and, I would argue, not for the better.

The then-and-now differences in how below-the-line money affects dealers are stark in at least four critical ways.

First, the checks I received as a dealer seem paltry in comparison to the size of factory checks today. Depending on the program and size of a dealer, the checks can run six figures or even higher.

> **"I feel more like a circus monkey than a business owner. I'm constantly jumping through factory hoops."**

Second, factory use of below-the-line money to incentivize dealer behavior is far more prevalent and invasive. The incentive programs are far greater in number and variety today than in years past. They touch almost every aspect of dealer operations, including customer satisfaction, sales performance, and facilities. As a dealer friend put it recently, "I feel more like a circus monkey than a business owner. I'm constantly jumping through factory hoops."

Third, below-the-line money is much more conditional than it used to be. In my day as a dealer, the customer satisfaction and sales programs were essentially available to every dealer. On the sales side, we earned the bonus if we sold any cars, and we earned more per car (often retroactive to the first car we sold) if we met or surpassed the factory targets. Only the worst dealers among us failed to get *some* bonus money.

Now, below-the-line programs typically follow an all-or-nothing formula. They require dealers to reach a minimum performance standard before they can earn any money. With stair-step programs, if you reach the sales target, you earn x dollars per car. If you exceed the target, you earn more per car for every sold unit.

But what happens if a dealer misses the factory-set target? Every dealer knows the answer. They get nothing. Nada. Zero. Zip. A goose egg.

Finally, and perhaps most significantly, below-the-line money is no longer gravy. It's become operationally necessary for most dealers to keep the showroom doors open.

In January 2014, the accounting group AutoTeam America released a report, "2025 Dealership Vision: What Lies Ahead!" The group found that 67 percent of dealers "make their income from the dealership below the line." The group also reported that many dealers believe the reliance on below-the-line money for profitability will only grow over the next decade.

As I think about the evolution of below-the-line money, I can't help but regard it as a quiet killer of the car business that has forever changed the entrepreneurial nature of owning a dealership.

Dealers no longer make money by satisfying customers and selling cars in the manner that best suits them. Instead, they make money by constantly working to satisfy factory requirements; the art and science of selling new vehicles has become a secondary, largely profitless, exercise.

Simply put, this isn't the car business I grew up in, and I'm not the only one who doesn't like it.

HOW BELOW-THE-LINE MONEY HURTS DEALERS

You could make a decent case that below-the-line money had a rather benign and benevolent beginning.

When I was a dealer, below-the-line money had fewer strings attached, and it tended to drive outcomes nearly every dealer could support—improving relationships with customers and selling more cars.

Both objectives fit squarely into my sense of place and purpose as a dealer. We truly cared about our customers, and we were always hungry to sell more cars. I'm pretty confident most of my dealer peers at the time felt the same way. After all, it wasn't that difficult to make the money, and, in order to receive it, we didn't have to do things that ran contrary to what we perceived as right for our businesses and ourselves.

But I don't think you could say the same today.

Take the stair-step programs factories routinely use to meet their market share and sales volume objectives. Factories have positioned these programs as a way to restore lost dealership profitability when they make adjustments to invoice prices or the manufacturer's suggested retail price (MSRP). Typically, the adjustments narrow the front-end margin potential for dealers.

But I would argue that the programs are more repressive than restorative, thanks largely to their all-or-nothing nature.

Consider the experience of a prominent Chrysler Dodge Jeep dealer in the Southwest. Among manufacturers, Chrysler has been more aggressive than others in using stair-step programs as a way to move metal.

The dealer says the prospect of earning, or losing out on, the below-the-line money makes dealers do stupid things.

On any given day, dealers across the country sell new vehicles at significant losses to meet the factory targets and earn stair-step incentive money. "There are times you work to hit the numbers so you can be profitable," the dealer says. "That's when you start giving cars away. We'll lose $5,000 to make $25,000."

> "On any given day, dealers across the country sell new vehicles at significant losses to meet the factory targets and earn stair-step incentive money."

To be sure, dealers don't like the idea of giving away vehicles, but they feel like they don't have a choice. If competitors give away cars to earn the factory bonus, the competitive nature of the business forces other dealers to do the same.

"It's a no-win situation," says a Midwest Chevrolet dealer.

"I can choose to stay out of the race to the bottom. But if I do, my cars will be overpriced in the market. Customers will go somewhere else for the better price, and I will lose out on the bonus money. It's a vicious cycle where the tail always wags the dog."

This cycle doesn't just affect dealers today—it carries over to tomorrow's buyers and the front-end margins on the vehicles they purchase, too.

Study after study affirms that new vehicle buyers don't really trust dealers or their prices. As a result, they check Edmunds .com, Kelley Blue Book, TrueCar, or other sources to determine a fair price for a new vehicle.

What do they see? Transaction prices that reflect all the stupid things dealers did to sell cars and earn factory bonus checks.

I'm hard-pressed to see how this is good for the car business.

But it gets even better, or worse, depending on your perspective.

The end result of these below-the-line programs today is highly ironic. The very programs that factories intended as a way to benefit dealership profitability actually make it worse, from a front-end gross perspective. In practice, the below-the-line money *encourages* the erosion of dealer margins, as we discussed in the last chapter, at a time when the decline of front-end grosses needs no encouragement.

I sometimes wonder why dealers aren't completely up in arms about the harmful effects stair-step programs create for their businesses. Then, I remember: Many dealers need the incentive money to stay in business, and it's tough to bite the hand that feeds you.

But some dealers are fighting back. I'm aware of at least one pending lawsuit where a dealer group, using recent updates to state franchise laws, contends that stair-step programs violate federal law that prohibits two-tier pricing. Factories are supposed to charge the same price for new vehicles to every dealer.

The dealers believe that the design of stair-step programs gives an innate advantage to larger dealers, who can use their size and scale to offer bigger discounts on cars to attract customers, earn bigger bonus payouts from factories, and, in turn, effectively purchase vehicles from factories at a lower price.

Even the National Automobile Dealers Association (NADA) has weighed in on the issue. In the past, it's urged factories to ensure that their below-the-line programs are "fair and available to all dealers, regardless of sales volume and dealership location."

To be honest, I have my doubts whether the pushback from dealers will be enough to cause any fundamental changes to the use of below-the-line money by manufacturers and the harmful effects this change to the car business creates for dealers.

No matter what, factories will do whatever is necessary to meet their market share and sales objectives—even if they make life, and profitability, more difficult for their dealer partners.

If I were a dealer today, I'd make it a priority to keep a close eye on factory expectations and find my own path to success:

Keep a close eye on factory expectations

Some dealers are more circumspect about the requirements factories write into their below-the-line programs than others. They push back when factories rework the boundaries of their primary marketing area (PMA) in a manner that doesn't make sense. They question factory expectations for increased sales volumes or facility upgrades when the current product lineup lacks the freshness and excitement that might win future buyers. Dealers may not have as much leverage with the factories as they'd like, but I'm told that dealers who push back when necessary do find occasional accommodation that can provide a better shot at achieving their objectives while satisfying factory requirements.

Find my own path to success

At their core, the factory programs that provide below-the-line money to dealers are all about compliance and conformity. The opportunity for dealers in the years ahead, it seems to me, rests with the way they choose to individualize the vehicle purchase experience with customers. We know they want more convenience, respect, and transparency as they shop for new vehicles. The key to future success lies in delivering on these expectations in a way that's unique to you. As the old saying goes, "If you take care of your customers, they'll have better reason to take care of you."

In the next chapter, we'll explore why the car business makes it difficult for dealers to convince customers that they truly have their best interests in mind.

3

TODAY'S TRANSPARENCY CHALLENGE: FACTORIES, DEALERS, AND FUZZY MATH

L et's face it: Consumers don't like to buy cars from dealers. We see this reality time and again in multiple industry studies. Here are two recent examples:

- Only seventeen out of four thousand vehicle buyers (a mere .4 percent) prefer the current buying process, according to Autotrader's "Car Buyer of the Future Study."

- Ninety-nine percent of consumers expect a hassle from the dealer when they want to buy a car, according to the DrivingSales' "Consumer Experience Research Study."

Such findings beg the questions—why is the perception of car buying so bad? And, how can dealers make it better? Let's tackle each one.

A POOR PERCEPTION BUILT FROM THE BEGINNING

To properly understand current consumer perceptions of car buying, it's worth taking a trip back in time. The seeds of today's fully mature dysfunction between buyers and dealers owes to the dawn of the car business in the early 1900s.

Back then, automakers like Henry Ford had product but they lacked an efficient way to sell their vehicles to the buying public.

According to a 2006 series on the franchise system by *Automotive News*, Ford and other automakers cut deals with existing local businesses, such as bicycle and buggy stores, to serve as distributors and retailers to move the metal. Ford also established company branches in cities across the country.

For dealers, the first two to three decades of automotive retailing proved both challenging and rewarding. The challenges often came from the factories themselves. The *Automotive News* series notes that Ford was notorious for relying on dealers to help factories make ends meet.

Following World War I, Ford "started dumping cars on dealers" and threatened to terminate their franchises if they refused.

Ford also set up factory stores to directly compete with dealers who weren't meeting performance expectations.

In this era, dealers must have felt pressure to perform. They often operated under one- or two-year agreements with their factory partners, and these covenants effectively allowed factories to terminate dealers without a just cause.

But the car business was coming into its own. Demand was stronger than supply, and the upside of operating a dealership apparently outweighed the risks dealers felt from factories. More dealers wanted in, rather than out.

World War II brought significant changes to the relationship between factories and dealers, as well as dealers and their customers.

The war wasn't kind to the dealer network. The *Automotive News* series notes that "The US auto industry went out of business for three and a half years" after the bombing of Pearl Harbor. The number of General Motors dealers declined by 20 percent during the war, as "auto plants became war plants."

As the war ended, the dealers who had found a way to remain in business had an opportunity to flourish, and they did.

With factory production shifting back to cars and pent-up demand from buyers who wanted new vehicles, dealers were in a retailing sweet spot, and they took full advantage of it.

The following nuggets from the *Automotive News* series highlight how the post–World War II era may have been the apex of dealers having the upper hand with buyers:

Price control

There weren't any price sticker laws or regulations. Dealers dictated what cars would cost their customers. Demand was so strong that customers rarely took issue. They paid the price dealers wanted them to pay.

Price packing

With essentially full control of vehicle pricing, dealers were known to pack the price of a new vehicle to make up for an overallowance on a trade. Buyers left thinking they got a great deal on their trade-in, while not realizing they'd overpaid for their new car.

Waiting lists

I can remember only one or two times that we had a waiting list for incoming inventory from the factory. But in the late 1940s, they were the norm, and dealers took advantage. The *Automotive News* series notes that "If you were No. 200 on the list, some well-placed cash might move you up to No. 15 or No. 25."

This was the situation that percolated until the mid-1950s.

By then, automakers and dealers had satisfied the pent-up demand for new cars following the war. Production outstripped demand, and factories pushed their dealers even harder to move the vehicles they continued to produce.

The dysfunction between dealers and their factory partners, and dealers and their customers, finally reached a boiling point, according to *Automotive News*.

Congress took action, creating legislation that afforded dealers greater protections in their factory agreements. Lawmakers also created a law that required sticker price disclosures, and, today, those stickers bear the name of former US Senator Mike Monroney (D-OK).

Looking back, I think it's fair to say that the early years of the car business involved a lot of gamesmanship between factories and dealers, as well as dealers and customers, that lives on today.

Taken together, you could make the case that factories created an environment where dealers may have felt forced to play the game with their customers. But you also can't ignore the reality that dealers took advantage of the situation for their own benefit.

> "The early years of the car business involved a lot of gamesmanship between factories and dealers, as well as dealers and customers, that lives on today."

In the end, it took congressional action to force a higher degree of transparency into the car business. Unfortunately, in the years since the congressional action, transparency remains elusive, and, at least in the eyes of consumers, dealers still have the upper hand.

One of the key reasons transparency remains elusive rests with the way factories have fundamentally changed the business for dealers.

As we discussed in the previous chapter, dealers today don't really make their money off the actual sale of a new vehicle; rather, the dealer's payback arrives below the line in the form of payments for meeting ever-more exacting customer satisfaction, facilities, sales, and service requirements.

There's a glaring irony in this fundamental shift for the car business. In many cases, the factories claimed that their adjustments to invoice prices and the manufacturer's suggested retail prices (MSRP) would mean *more* transparency for buyers. I would argue, however, that the exact opposite has occurred.

Today, as new vehicle buyers go online, they see the cumulative effects of the below-the-line money as they research cars and dealer asking prices.

Some dealers include consumer incentives in their new vehicle prices, others don't. Some dealers include prospective stairstep bonus money in their prices, others don't. Some only apply stairsteps as they close deals. Meanwhile, other dealers do their best to keep stair-step incentive money strictly below the line, posting only the MSRP.

Of course, this dynamic varies across manufacturers, as some require MSRP- or above invoice-only pricing.

But the result for buyers is universal: It's nearly impossible to determine how much they might have to pay for a new vehicle without contacting the dealership. And, when they do make contact, most dealers require buyers to come into the dealership to work out deal terms.

As this occurs, the long-standing, poor perception of car buying continues to grow, and dealers pay the price.

Take, for instance, sites like TrueCar. Its message of greater pricing transparency, and a hassle-free experience, plays directly to consumers' car-buying perceptions. It creates a situation where dealers essentially complete deals on terms set by a third party and pay extra for the privilege.

Over time, it seems to me that the opportunity for dealers rests in making the promise of a positive, transparent experience a reality online and in their showrooms. Then, little by little, we'll see consumer car-buying perceptions change, with the benefits rolling to where they belong, with dealers.

In the end, dealers have too much at stake in their businesses, and their communities, to always be viewed as the bad guys whenever someone wants to buy a car.

4

FROM THE UPPER HAND TO THE GIVING HAND

t'd be nice if every car buyer today understood how bad things used to be in our industry. Dealers often made a killing, and customers were none the wiser. It was deal making at its least transparent—where only a select few really knew if they got a decent deal or they'd been fleeced by a dealer.

Perhaps if today's buyers understood how bad the gamesmanship used to be, they'd feel better that car buying today is, at the very least, a little more transparent.

But we can dream all we want.

Consumer attitudes and beliefs are what they are. In the buyer's mind, dealers still have the upper hand. Their distrust is palpable and, if you look beyond the car business at other retailers, perfectly understandable.

Consider how the Internet has dramatically shaped retail expectations for buyers and how dealers have (and have not yet) responded.

For today's consumers, the Internet has ushered in an unprecedented degree of ease and openness when it comes to buying anything and everything. With a few clicks, you can find what you want and the price you're expected to pay for virtually any product. You can easily see what other people think of the product and the retailer selling it.

For most items, you can complete a purchase from home or work and have it show up wherever you want it delivered. It's never been easier to be a well-informed and wise retail customer.

Retailers who thrive in this environment do so because they meet or exceed the more exacting expectations and preferences today's consumers have developed online. The retailers also thrive because they've learned that tradition-bound business practices often fall short of delivering the easy and transparent transaction consumers expect, whether it's completed online or in a physical store.

Unfortunately, for many dealers, the rise of the Internet and the transparency it requires has proven highly challenging.

To be sure, part of the challenge owes to the history of the car business, where manufacturers and a dearth of disclosure laws gave rise to a belief that providing little or no transparency is the best and only way for dealers to handle the business of selling cars to consumers.

You could see this belief in full bloom when the Internet first arrived. At the time, I was in the business of helping dealers post their inventory on third-party websites, as well as their own. Time after time, we'd run into dealers who hotly debated whether it was right and proper to post vehicles, let alone prices, online.

Such reactions underscored the prevailing belief that prices should only be shared in the showroom, lest a consumer take what they see online and shop somewhere else.

The Internet also gave rise to other suspicions. Some dealers viewed the Internet as a threat to their very existence—a virtual pipeline that would disintermediate them and give factories an avenue to sell vehicles directly to consumers.

Over time, such stiff resistance gave way, grudgingly, to a new reality. Dealers really do need to market and merchandise vehicles online and include prices.

This reluctant recognition then led to a bifurcated business model: Many dealers put cars and prices online, but they had separate prices, and sales processes, for customers in the showroom.

I don't think it's a stretch to say that many dealers are still emerging from this inefficient and less-than-transparent business practice. There are still Internet-only specials. And there are still plenty of dealerships where it really doesn't matter what price a potential buyer saw online, even if they found it on the dealer's own website.

But here's the rub: These kinds of pricing and sales tactics put off buyers who are increasingly accustomed to buying everything with a minimal degree of friction and a maximum degree of ease and transparency.

I've thought long and hard about this dichotomy. In light of overwhelming evidence that suggests dealers would do a lot better if they simply gave buyers what they desire, why do dealers continue to resist doing so?

The answer to this question, I believe, owes to the tradition-bound idea that dealers should always retain the upper hand when dealing with a vehicle buyer—that buyers can't possibly know the precise car they'll need, or the one they can afford, without sitting down in a showroom with an associate and walking down the road to a sale.

Unfortunately, this thinking runs counter to every bit of evidence, and every online retailing trend, that has emerged in recent years. We now know that

- Vehicle buyers visit less than two dealerships in person before they make a purchase—a pretty significant indicator, I think, that buyers don't feel the need, or desire, to go there unless and until they must.

- Seventy-two percent of buyers want to spend less time in the dealership to complete a transaction. This finding is no surprise given the insight above.

- Fifty-six percent of buyers want to begin working part of their vehicle deal transaction online, and 45 percent want to remain anonymous until they lock in a deal. This data from Autotrader shouldn't surprise anyone who has purchased anything online. These vehicle buyer desires mirror the shopping process most, if not all, major online retailers offer on their sites.

- "Trust and responsiveness trump price" with today's buyers, according to DrivingSales data.

- Fifty-six percent of buyers would purchase again from a dealer who provided the experience they preferred, according to Autotrader.

- A majority of buyers still want to negotiate their new or used vehicle purchases. Ask any one-price dealer, and they'll confirm that more than half of their customers ask for discounts, despite all the advertising and "why buy here" collateral that says the price you see is the price you pay.

When you wrap all these insights together, it becomes pretty clear that upper-hand-minded dealers are increasingly (and sometimes desperately) playing a losing hand.

Think about it: The findings reflect the fact that today's new and used vehicle buyers are hungry for a different experience—one that largely takes place online and offers a higher degree of ease, efficiency, and transparency than they encountered the last time they, or an influential someone in their circle, purchased a vehicle.

Broadly speaking, today's buyers expect dealers to give them more information and understanding about a vehicle, and its purchase price and terms, without having to go to a dealership and deal with someone who's paid to put the pace of discovery on the dealer's terms, not the customer's.

Digital retailing experts express these new expectations this way:

Buyers want dealers to truly make the first offer. They want price and payment information delivered to them in a manner that fits their busy lifestyles and technology preferences. They also prefer anonymity, at least during initial stages of vetting a vehicle and a dealer, and they'd like to do these things from the comfort of their own homes and offices.

I like to summarize these expectations by saying buyers want dealers to offer a giving hand, and they want to see the first signs of it online.

Dealers who begin to meet these customer expectations are really doing the relationship-building that's been a part of the car business for one hundred years. The difference is that these initial stages of engagement, understanding, and trust occur online rather than in the showroom.

It's also true that dealers who do not provide this expectation-meeting experience run the risk of turning away potential buyers, even if they have the exact car the buyer wants in stock.

THREE STEPS TO EXTEND YOUR GIVING HAND

It's important to note that digital retailing experts aren't recommending that dealers go all out and build an online shopping experience along the lines of Amazon.

To be sure, there are some customers who would like a "buy it now" option online to purchase their next new or used vehicle. But those buyers are a small minority of the overall vehicle-buying public.

The vast majority of buyers—up to 90 percent by some estimates—recognize that car deals are complex and require physically engaging dealers to complete their vehicle purchases. These buyers would like a process that enables them to complete most, if not all, of their next car deal online and to eliminate the surprise and uncertainties they've learned to loathe from the last time they bought a car.

To satisfy these buyers, the experts recommend that dealers reexamine the way they are currently engaging and communicating with customers online and eliminate the tactics and tricks that reflect a traditional upper-hand deal-making mentality.

The experts recommend the following three steps to help dealers build a more efficient, transparent process for meeting the expectations and needs of buyers today and tomorrow.

Step 1: Engage

Dealers can all pretty much agree that when a potential customer looks at a vehicle details page (VDP), it's perhaps the most significant expression of interest, if not intent, to purchase the vehicle that occurs online. Buyers click on VDPs to look at pictures, read descriptions, and watch videos. The examination is really a pressure test: Do I like the way the car looks? Does it have the options I want? Do the condition and mileage seem OK? Does the price fit the parameters I found on third-party valuation sites?

For many dealers, this pressure test is the beginning of the end of their engagement with a potential buyer. The experience typically starts to unravel when the customer begins interacting with the VDP itself, clicking on payment calculators or trade-in valuation tools to begin speccing out their deal terms.

The problem? These tools typically ask the customers to give up their contact information before they get the information they seek. And, in some cases, the tools aren't really meant to give deal-ready information anyway; they're meant to generate leads.

Dealers can tell if the tools they offer undermine a positive engagement with potential buyers by assessing bailout rates. I'm told it's not uncommon for less than 30 percent of customers who try these tools to actually use them fully.

Digital retailing experts note that when buyers can easily get the answers they want on specific deal terms (e.g., price, down payment, monthly payment, interest rate, and trade-in valuation) without being forced to provide contact and other personal information, they are more likely to voluntarily engage the dealership. So begins the process of building confidence and trust.

The experts also say that dealers are often surprised when they go first and enable tools that give customers what they seek on their terms. The dealers find that customers are more honest about credit scores and the condition of their trade-ins. Why? Because they are more at ease and more likely to tell the truth.

Step 2: Communicate

Industry studies suggest that dealers never hear from a majority of their new or used vehicle buyers before they show up at the dealership, inquiring about a specific vehicle.

To me, this dynamic suggests that buyers fully know what to expect if they do call, email, or initiate a chat with a dealer: They'll get prodded and pushed to set an appointment, and they won't get the answers they want about the vehicle they found online—even if it's a simple question about whether the car's in stock.

Dealers should really ask themselves three questions:

1. What's the goal of our initial conversation with a customer—to sell the appointment or to make it easier for the individual to buy our car?

2. Do the people I empower to communicate with customers have the ability, background, and information to accurately answer customer questions or, if they don't, to quickly get the answers?

3. To what degree do these communications reflect any understanding of where customers left off online?

As dealers ask these questions, they typically start to see areas where they can improve the giving hand they extend to customers in their communications and eliminate the off-putting disconnects many buyers currently feel between their online and in-dealership engagements.

Step 3: Automate

You might consider the automation of vehicle purchases the last frontier for dealers who embrace the giving-hand approach to engaging buyers. Given the nature of car deals, I suspect there will always be some element of one-to-one interaction, even if it doesn't occur in person.

But the race is on to provide dealers technology and tools that will help them facilitate F&I transactions online—and meet buyer expectations for efficiency and transparency.

These efforts follow research that shows nearly 85 percent of buyers would like to know more about F&I products before they get to a dealership, and nearly two-thirds of buyers say they'd be more likely to purchase F&I products if they had the opportunity to explore or research them online.

In the near term, these findings suggest that it'll be important for dealers to at least provide some level of access to their current F&I offerings and the value proposition they provide to potential buyers.

Long term, I see these efforts to automate F&I purchase transactions as a positive on two levels.

First, it will squarely address consumer desires to spend less time in the dealership. We all know that dealers often require buyers, who've already agreed to purchase a vehicle, wait thirty, forty-five, or even sixty minutes to see an F&I manager. With automation, dealers can offer sign and go F&I transactions that customers initiate online and finalize in the showroom. Most dealers would agree that if they could eliminate the all-too-frequent F&I bottlenecks, it'd be good for everybody.

Second, automation helps dealers facilitate increased efficiency, productivity, and profitability of individual F&I managers. Early research indicates that when dealers properly facilitate F&I deals online, they make as much or more on a per-deal basis as they do from deals completed in the "box." At the same time, F&I managers could work more deals in less time—an outcome that's in complete harmony with every dealer's need to sell more vehicles more efficiently to maximize profitability and their return on investment.

After reading this chapter, some dealers may be asking, "Will a giving hand really result in selling more cars and making more money?"

Hopefully, the next chapter helps properly answer the question.

5

BUYING A CAR IN THE NOT-TOO-DISTANT FUTURE

The setting: A franchise dealership, somewhere in America, a little before 10:00 a.m. A vehicle drives into the dealership lot and parks near the door. A man enters the showroom. A sales associate approaches.

Sam, the sales associate (extending his right hand): "Good morning, Bill! It's great to see you this morning. I'm Sam, the guy who's been working with you on your purchase of your new car. Did you see it parked outside?"

Bill (shaking the associate's hand): "Good morning, Sam. It's good to meet you in person. I didn't notice the car outside. But I'm curious: How did you know it was me when I walked in here?"

Sam (laughing): "Well, I looked you up online and saw your picture. I also got a text message when you came on the lot—a technology we use to make sure we are ready to serve customers like you when you arrive. Can I get the keys to your trade-in? My colleague Chris is ready to check out the car and make sure everything's as you described it online."

Bill (handing over the keys): "Here you go. That's interesting about the technology. Is there an app like that for parents?"

Sam (chuckling): "Funny you should mention that. Your new vehicle does include the geo-tracking package you indicated you wanted online. That'll help you know who's using the vehicle and where they go. We'll check that out in a minute. Why don't you take a seat here. Want some coffee? Cream and sugar?"

Bill (sitting down): "Sure, I'd love some coffee. Black is fine. Thank you."

(Sam returns with coffee and an iPad.)

Sam: "OK, Bill. Here's your coffee. Now, I know I promised that we'd have you out of here, with your new vehicle, in forty-five minutes. So let's review all the things we did online, OK?"

Bill (checking his phone for the time): "Sure, that'd be great. Am I still going to get $5,000 for my trade-in and get the new car for $43,780?"

Sam: "It'll be up to Chris to verify the trade-in offer. That's really the only variable because we have to physically evaluate the vehicle. He should be back in a few minutes. Everything else is exactly as we agreed—purchase price of $43,780; a $2,000 down payment; a five-year finance deal at $481 a month, with an interest rate of 5 percent; the Platinum service package you requested, which includes lifetime oil changes and washes; and the geo-tracking technology. It's all here on the iPad. Why don't you take a few moments to review it, and I'll text Chris to check the status of your trade-in."

(Sam hands Bill the iPad and sends a text. Bill flips through and reviews the deal documents for a few minutes, then looks up.)

Bill (handing the iPad to Sam): "This all looks good to me."

Sam: "Perfect. Thank you. I just got word from Chris. He says everything checks out except for the tires. They're more worn than we thought they'd be. He'd like to show you what he found, since he's estimating it'll change our offer to $4,600. Shall we head outside?"

Bill: "Nah. No need. I wasn't too sure about saying the tires were in 'good' condition. They've been on the car awhile. $4,600 is fine."

Sam: "OK, great. Let me adjust the trade-in allowance. Should we add the difference for the tires to your down payment or include it as part of your loan?"

Bill: "Let's do the down payment."

Sam: "OK. One moment, please."

(Sam works on the iPad and hands it to Bill.)

Sam (pointing to the iPad screen): "OK. Here's where I updated the deal terms. See, there's the new trade-in allowance at $4,600 and, over here, your down payment is now $2,400. Everything else is exactly the same. Does this look OK?"

Bill: "Looks good to me."

Sam (checking his watch): "Great. It's 10:20 right now. How about we go check out your new car to make sure it's all OK, and then we'll come back here, sign the deal, and get you on the road."

Bill (looking at his watch): "You really are going to have me out of here in forty-five minutes, aren't you?"

Sam (smiling): "C'mon, Bill. You should know me by now. I told you when we first chatted online that we're all straight shooters here. You wanted to be in and out in forty-five minutes, and that's what we're going to do. Let's go soak up some new car smell, shall we?"

Bill: "Let's do it. And I was only kidding about the forty-five minutes. It's just that this whole experience is so much better than the last time I bought a car. I'm actually having fun."

Sam (opening the showroom door, patting Bill on the back, and laughing): "That makes two of us, Bill."

———

Does this scenario strike you as a bit far-fetched?

It shouldn't.

While the interaction between Sam and Bill is fictional, it's based on the ways progressive dealers today are reinventing their sales processes to create more positive, transparent, and trust-based purchase experiences for their new and used vehicle buyers: Bill basically worked the deal on his own time, using tools Sam and his dealer provided.

Sam knew the ins and outs of the deal. Their first meet-and-greet picked up exactly where they'd left things online.

There really wasn't any friction—even when Sam essentially called out Bill for overstating the condition of the tires on the trade-in.

Bill trusts Sam. He might even like him. This trust compelled him to do the right thing on the tires and the extra $400.

Bill will probably tell his friends, in person and on social media, about his experience. No doubt, he'll send along Sam's name if asked.

Bill sold himself on the service contract, the geo-location app, and the terms of the loan deal. Sam may or may not get a piece of the action on these deal elements. Either way, the dealer's happy to pay less than a traditional F&I commission.

Bill was in and out of the dealership in forty-five minutes, as promised.

Bill will probably show up, as scheduled, and possibly without prompting, for a first service visit.

It's these kind of positive customer experience outcomes that have dealers across the country, both large and small, retooling the way they sell cars.

Most of the large dealer groups are headed in this direction. They've made significant investments in one-price, one-person, online-driven deal making. Some of these are still experimental, but others are on their way to larger scale.

Dozens of smaller dealers have adopted a one-price model for both new and used vehicles. They may not have all the online deal-making tools of better-invested competitors, but they're doing everything they can to provide the faster, more transparent experience buyers today, and tomorrow, desire.

Even some original equipment manufacturers (OEM) are in on this game of giving customers a better, more efficient, and online-driven experience. For example, in 2016, Lexus launched its no-haggle-pricing program, and Cadillac unveiled its Pinnacle Program, which calls for virtual store-driven purchases at some dealerships.

Both programs have met stiff resistance from dealers. To be sure, I also question the degree to which OEMs should dictate the ins and outs of deal making on dealer websites and showrooms. Nonetheless, the fact that the desire to craft a more positive buying experience exists at the OEM level is telling.

Perhaps the biggest question in all of this is whether the investment and reinvention in a more positive buyer experience will provide a sufficient return to dealers.

If you talk to AutoNation or Sonic Automotive executives, they'd say it is. They are expanding, rather than backing away from, their vision for a new way of retailing.

The same goes for the vast majority of dealers I know who have gone to a one-price model or have taken the initial steps to make digital retailing a working reality at their dealerships. They are all in on these investments. They see them as essential, evolutionary steps to remain viable as retailers.

"In another ten to twenty years, I think we'll largely be a delivery service as a dealer," says a Midwest Honda dealer who has adopted the giving-hand strategy discussed in the previous chapter. In 2017, their goal is to work more deals online, further reduce transaction times (which run forty-five minutes to an hour for customers who begin vehicle purchases online), and continue to give buyers the experience they want.

"Everything we're doing today is a step toward a different retailing future," the dealer says. "We've gained an additional fifteen to twenty deals a month, and they gross more than our more traditional sales. If you ask me why, I think it's because we offer something other dealers around here don't."

> **"In another ten to twenty years, I think we'll largely be a delivery service as a dealer."**

I realize some dealers see things differently. They believe, deeply, that more traditional selling methods remain the best way to retail vehicles.

But I would urge these dealers to consider how much the

industry is already moving in this direction and how quickly the shift to a more customer-driven, online-enabled purchase experience is occurring. Over time, it seems to me that the traditional beliefs will increasingly become barriers to future success.

6

MAKING YOUR PEOPLE A HIGHER PRIORITY

I t's amazing to think about how much dealers invest in their employees and how poorly many manage this investment.

You might even consider dealers' human capital management as the greatest investment inefficiency in the car business today.

According to NADA, dealers collectively spend $58.1 billion on employees—a tally that translates to an annual expense of more than $3.5 million for the average dealership. Few dealers would disagree that personnel costs are their single biggest expense, and an even greater worry, on a cash flow basis, than the costs of advertising, facilities, and inventory.

But here's what strikes me as highly problematic. Employee turnover in dealerships is pervasive, and it's getting worse.

In late 2015, NADA released the results of an annual workforce study that shows turnover for sales associates runs 71 percent, up 5 percent from the prior year. In service, turnover for service advisors runs 41 percent, up 4.5 percent. In F&I, turnover among F&I managers is 37 percent, up 5 percent.

The data also shows that turnover among managers, while not as chronic as other customer-facing, front-line positions, runs about 26 percent for sales managers and 16 percent for general managers.

Some may find some good news in the NADA data. Total dealership turnover ran 39 percent in 2015 (up 3 percent from the prior year), which is 5 percent less than federal Bureau of Labor Statistics estimates for turnover across all private sector business.

But that's like saying, "Hey, look! We didn't finish last so we're doing OK!"

I would beg to differ. To me, the rampant pace of employee turnover is extremely close to being an industry embarrassment, and it represents the single-biggest issue facing dealers as they operate in a market that will continue to compress margins and profitability as sales volumes normalize in the coming years.

At some level, you have to ask, how is it possible that turnover in dealerships could be so bad if dealers pay decent wages and the nation, as a whole, isn't fully employed?

NADA offers a possible answer: "The high turnover rate of

sales consultants can be attributed to two factors. First, this represents many entry-level workers who decided to try sales but then realized they did not like it. Second, automotive retailing is going through major industry changes, which is putting pressure on sales staff earnings."

Both points are unquestionably true. But I would submit that the *real* answer behind the persistent turnover problems has more to do with the first point than the second.

Let's drill down.

First, I doubt that most entry-level workers are accepting job offers from dealers to simply try the position. I have to believe that the vast majority are signing up to actually work. Most are also likely to be excited by the opportunity, particularly if they're coming from positions with less pay and potential.

Second, the rate of turnover suggests that something goes terribly wrong, pretty quickly, between the new employee and the dealership that provided the job.

Maybe the person wasn't cut out for the job. Maybe someone set unrealistic expectations for the new employee. Maybe the employee and his or her manager didn't get along.

But guess what? It seems to me that the ultimate responsibility for any or all of these potential mismatches rests with the dealer or manager that made the hire.

I simply can't believe that job candidates are signing up for gigs for which they have no aptitude or interest. And even if they are, isn't it the responsibility of the dealership to weed out these individuals before they become part of the team?

My apologies if I'm sounding a bit strident. But I'm a little bit like a reformed cigarette smoker when it comes to human capital management or, put more simply, hiring and firing people.

You see, during my time as a dealer, I suffered the same turnover problems that persist today. I can't remember how many nights I lost sleep because I was worried that someone else would quit, that we wouldn't have enough people to fill our showroom shifts the next day, and that I'd have to spend even more time going through resumes and interviews.

I'm absolutely certain I gained a few gray hairs due to employee turnover. It was a constant battle.

I remember interviewing a guy who'd proudly claimed to be a "fifteen-car guy with a five-pound Rolodex" who would help light up our showroom with his loyal customers. I liked him a lot and hired him on the spot.

> "I didn't check references. I didn't do a background check or drug test. I didn't even introduce him to the sales manager. I said, 'Let's go!'"

But here's what I didn't do: I didn't check references. I didn't do a background check or drug test. I didn't even introduce him to the sales manager. I said, "Let's go!" He said, "OK!"

You can probably guess the outcome. He was gone soon after the draw ran out. His fifteen-car production proved to be less than half that. I can't remember ever seeing the Rolodex he bragged about.

Unfortunately, this example played over and over again, like the proverbial needle skipping on a broken record. It defined the way we hired at our dealership—way more desperation than discipline. A track record of charmers who turned out to be chumps.

It's fair to ask why we didn't stop ourselves. After all, the definition of insanity is doing the same thing over and over again and expecting different results.

The answer is that we didn't regard the seemingly nonstop pace of hiring and firing as anything other than the nature of the car business. We didn't think, for a moment, that we had a faulty approach to the way we brought people on board. We just thought the green peas couldn't cut it.

Twenty-plus years later, I now recognize how much I missed the boat as a boss and businessman. I can only wonder how many more cars we might have sold, and how much more money I would have made, if I knew then what I know today about human capital management.

LESSONS TO LEAVE THE LEGACY OF LAXITY BEHIND

You might say that I see a lot of myself in the current employee turnover rates at dealerships. The legacy of lax hiring decisions and retention processes unfortunately lives on. It is for this reason that I feel the need to sound the alarm.

You see, some dealers really get it. They rightfully think it's crazy to put up with perpetual turnover or think *That's just the way it is in the car business.*

They've tightened their hiring processes. They've taken the time to truly figure out what they stand for as dealers and employers and to align every hiring decision to the mission and values they've created.

They recognize that career paths and work culture matter more today than ever before. They've made work hours more compatible with the desires of Millennials, moms, and others. They've changed compensation plans to reflect the proper belief that everyone should know what they can expect to make in a given month.

These dealers think of hiring and retention much differently than I did. For them, it's not the "soft stuff" of running a dealership. Rather, improved employee hiring and retention now stands as a differentiating strategy for their future relevance, success, and profitability as auto retailers.

In many ways, these dealers are lighting the path forward for the rest of the industry. They are demonstrating that high turnover rates aren't an inevitable by-product of a highly competitive, sometimes chaotic business.

No, these dealers view high turnover and low retention as a choice. You either accept it or you don't.

The best part of all, however, is that these dealers aren't shy about their achievement of putting their people first and recognizing that you really do need committed, happy employees to turn out happy, satisfied customers—to minimize inefficiencies and generate the fullest possible returns on their dealership investments.

How do they do it? Here are a few pointers I've gleaned from dealers and others on improved hiring and retention.

Assess yourself

The dealers all say their improvements in reducing employee turnover and increasing retention followed introspection. They looked in the mirror. They asked themselves and their key managers hard questions. What are the real root causes for our persistent turnover? What changes would help end the problem? What's our reputation as a dealer and employer? How can we improve both? What's our mission? How would we best describe our values as an organization?

Adam Robinson, CEO of Hireology, says this kind of self-assessment is an absolutely critical first step toward minimizing, if not eliminating, persistent turnover.

"Self-assessment is like the foundation of a house. It supports everything you build on top of it," Robinson says. "It shapes the questions you should ask of every job candidate. It feeds the type of culture or work environment you're trying to build. It directs the career paths and training you implement. It helps keep the good people you hire happy to be working for you."

Be consistent

I know for a fact that I never asked the same interview questions of every job candidate or used the same criteria for promotions.

I made it up as I went along, based on what I thought was fair, necessary, and reasonable. "Things haven't changed all that much," Robinson said. "Most dealerships aren't hiring based on defined criteria, asking the same questions of every candidate to help quantify whether they have the characteristics for success."

I asked him to define the criteria. He said that dealers who screen candidates for a positive disposition toward work, a desire for accountability, performance-based work experience, and culture fit tend to find, hire, and keep better candidates.

"Dale, it's no different than pricing used vehicles. You know that if you follow a specific methodology and process, you will increase your chances of being better off. The same is true in hiring," he said.

Provide pathways for success

For each of the past three years, I've attended *Automotive News'* Best Dealerships To Work For event. I've considered it a must-attend event for what it represents for the automotive industry—a gathering of bright star dealers who are a whole lot smarter than I ever was about employee hiring and retention.

Nearly every dealer who took the stage to share their efforts to improve hiring and retention pointed to defined career paths and related training opportunities as critical to their success. These dealers don't view the costs of such individual development and training as anything other than a sound investment in the future health of their businesses.

The dealers also say that offering these opportunities is especially important among Millennials, who made up 48 percent of new hires at dealerships in 2014, according to NADA.

There is, of course, a lot more to the story of how dealers can stop the persistent pace of turnover. I, for one, believe that it needs to happen sooner rather than later, given the current climate of margin compression and sales plateaus.

I would challenge every dealer to reduce their ninety-day and one-year turnover rates by 10 percent in the next twelve months and then build on those improvements.

You must ask how soon can you turn your dealership into a truly people-first organization, and what will the consequences be, in terms of missed opportunity, ongoing headaches, and less-than-optimal performance, the longer it takes you to get there?

7

A NEW PRESIDENT AND AUTO RETAIL REGULATION

There were a lot of dealers who celebrated the outcome of the 2016 presidential election. All of the dealers may not have liked how Donald Trump operated as a person or a businessman, but they shared a sense of satisfaction as a Republican retook the White House.

The dealers were hoping, of course, that the new president would provide them some relief from federal investigations and oversight of the car business.

Such hopes came from three developments that have given dealers, and their representatives in federal and state governments, cause for great concern.

DEVELOPMENT 1: F&I SCRUTINY

If you want to give dealers heartburn, just say, "Consumer Finance Protection Bureau" (CFPB).

Most dealers are already aware of the agency's interest in reducing dealer markups on finance deals. They saw the stories that highlighted how the CFPB has taken captive finance companies, like American Honda Financial Corporation, to task for their long-standing practice of allowing dealers to mark up interest rates on finance deals.

They have seen how the CFPB's investigations into allegedly discriminatory lending practices on the part of dealers and finance companies have resulted in caps on dealer markups and a shift to flat fees—all in an effort to avoid being the target of another CFPB investigation.

Dealers themselves have also become more aware of finance and insurance (F&I) compliance. The CFPB's investigations and oversight have spurred public groups like AutoNation and Sonic Automotive to stall plans to develop in-house financing operations—even though such ventures would likely benefit their retail businesses.

As one executive put it, "We don't want to open ourselves up for trouble."

For its part, the National Automobile Dealers Association (NADA) is fighting the CFPB.

NADA believes CFPB "issued guidance that threatens to eliminate a dealer's flexibility to offer consumers discounted auto loans. CFPB is attempting to change the $1 trillion auto loan market and limit market competition *without* prior public comment, using flawed statistics, and *without* analyzing the impact of the guidance on consumers."

Since a Republican president has taken office, there's been additional momentum behind NADA's efforts to rein in, if not eliminate altogether, the CFPB's investigation and oversight efforts.

But I worry that even with a Republican White House, and a Republican-controlled congress, the CFPB won't go away. In fact, I'm concerned that CFPB, or an agency like it, might get even more aggressive.

I say this because the CFPB is perceived by many outside retail automotive as a necessary federal agency with a near-noble cause—to protect consumers from the kind of financial flimflamming that resulted in the housing bubble that precipitated the Great Recession of 2008. Some also believe that the success of retail automotive in recent years has largely been driven by ready availability of financing, complete with extended loan terms, redefined loan to value ratios, and risk swaps.

"If dealers face an even greater level of F&I scrutiny, I'm concerned what investigators might find."

If dealers face an even greater level of F&I scrutiny, I'm concerned what investigators might find.

Here's why: We all know that for the past fifteen-plus years, front-end margins on new and used vehicles have steadily declined. We also know that dealers have exercised their right to lean on their F&I departments to increase production and profitability and make up the money they used to realize as front-end gross profit.

You see this trend in the NADA data: In 2002, F&I sales accounted for less than 25 percent of gross profit generated in the new and used vehicle departments. In 2016, F&I sales accounted for more than 40 percent of new and used vehicle department gross profits. Today, F&I penetration rates run near 90 percent for new vehicles and 85 percent for used vehicles— far higher benchmarks than I've ever seen. On a per-car basis, F&I income runs $2,000 for some dealers.

In this environment, one has to ask what the CFPB or some other entity might find if it began an in-depth look at how dealers present and sell F&I products.

Would they see a lot of disparity in the purchase prices from one customer to another? Would they see consistent offerings of the same products and related disclosures to every customer? Would they see any kind of correlation between the number of purchased products and customer credit scores or financing rates and other loan terms? Would they question the value of specific product offerings? Would they ask if the pay plans of F&I managers, who are often the highest-paid individuals in a dealership, incentivize behaviors that don't directly serve the interests or needs of buyers?

It's entirely possible that I'm overly worried. Maybe the CFPB will go away and another, similar organization won't ever rise up to take its place.

But, if I were still a dealer, I wouldn't be taking that bet.

I would be asking my F&I managers and myself these questions. I'd be taking my own steps to ensure a higher level of consistency and transparency in my F&I office, rather than counting on someone else to reduce the risk of liability on my behalf.

DEVELOPMENT 2: RECALL VEHICLES

As most dealers should be aware, 2016 brought two unprecedented actions related to recalls.

The first was American Honda Motor Company's factory-ordered stop sale on recalled used vehicles, issued in the wake of the Takata airbag recall. The second was AutoNation's decision to halt the sale of any used vehicle with an open recall until it received replacement parts and repaired the vehicle.

Let's tackle the Honda stop-sale order first.

Worried about additional airbag liability, Honda ordered its dealers to stop the sale of specific used vehicles. The order struck me as unprecedented in four ways.

First, the stop sale occurred before Honda had replacement parts in hand, and on the way to dealers, to fix the airbag inflator issue. This decision followed efforts by the National

Highway Transportation Safety Administration (NHSTA) to encourage more proactive efforts by manufacturers to notify vehicle owners of potential problems with their vehicles.

Second, the stop-sale order affects a sizable number of *used*, not new, vehicles. Acura dealers say as much as 40 percent of their used vehicle inventories were affected by the recalls. Honda dealers estimate the stop sale affected about 20 percent of their used vehicles.

In either case, the factory order means dealers will have dead capital tied up in these vehicles until replacement parts arrive, putting a crimp on their sales volumes unless they choose to replace the lost volume with off-brand units.

Third, while Honda has crafted a plan to compensate dealers for the stop-sale induced pain, their efforts to account for depreciation, floorplan assistance, "lot rot," storage fees, and other factors make dealers uncertain if they'll be made whole when replacement parts arrive and the stop sale ends. As one dealer put it, "It's better than nothing, but there's really no way to tell if it'll be enough." Part of the concern reflects the inevitable volatility that will come as the stop sale–affected vehicles get repaired and return to the market, not to mention the opportunity cost of capital tied up in stop-sale units.

Fourth, Honda included a stern warning for its dealers in its stop-sale order. "Should an unrepaired vehicle result in any claim because of the required recall repair, the dealership will be solely responsible to the claimant and will be required to defend and indemnify American Honda for any resulting claims."

It doesn't appear that Honda has needed to take any dealer to task for violating this provision. As such, we don't really know if Honda's effort to shift liability to its dealer partners holds any legal weight. Still, the provision is a stark reminder that factories will put their dealers on the hook if they determine it's in their best interests to do so.

Meanwhile, we also have AutoNation's noble effort to do more than current federal law requires and voluntarily stop retailing used vehicles with open recalls or sending them unrepaired to auction.

AutoNation began the effort in the summer of 2015, essentially saying it was the right thing to do in an era of large numbers of vehicles with faulty airbags and other problems.

After a few months, however, the company unwound the policy. In the spring of 2016, it decided to wholesale vehicles with an open recall if they found it would take longer than six months to obtain recall replacement parts. By the end of 2016, the company scrapped the policy altogether: If parts aren't immediately available, the dealer group retails or wholesales the vehicle with a window sticker disclaimer.

The final decision for AutoNation reportedly followed the presidential election. Executives reportedly figured any momentum the NHSTA might have gained at making recall efforts more effective and transparent would fizzle with the new administration.

Time will tell if the executives are correct. In the meantime, however, NADA is working to stop federal lawmakers from passing overbroad bills that would formally prohibit dealers from selling used vehicles with open recalls, even for off-brand units.

Citing J. D. Power stats, NADA says that grounding used vehicles affected by open recalls would hurt trade-in values for vehicle owners by as much as $4,000 to $5,000, with an average devaluation of $1,210. NADA also makes the point that many recalls do not represent safety hazards that would require the dramatic step of grounding the vehicle.

Perhaps the main takeaway is this: The recall landscape is shifting. We can expect ever-higher numbers of recalls as vehicles include ever-more complex operating systems and technologies. It seems wise to encourage dealers to at least recognize that recall vehicles, and the risks they represent, are fast becoming an everyday problem for everyone.

DEVELOPMENT 3: FRANCHISE LAWS

There were two events that occurred in 2016 that called into question, at least for me, if dealers could really count on state franchise laws to protect them the way they have in the past.

The first event occurred early in the year. The Federal Trade Commission held an exploratory hearing in February in Washington, DC, to examine the current franchised system and its effectiveness as a distribution network for new vehicles.

I wasn't at the hearing, but I'm told it didn't leave a favorable impression among dealers and their advocates who did attend.

I've heard the meeting described as "truly hostile" toward dealers. A dealer consultant thought the discussions revealed a view among academics and regulators that current franchise laws created an "obscene profit" for dealers that comes at an "intolerable, damaging cost to the consumer."

The second event involved Tesla. The rise of the electric car company in recent years has spurred multiple state dealer associations to seek tougher franchise law provisions to prohibit direct-to-consumer sales via factory-owned stores by auto manufacturers. Tesla has taken these provisions to court in multiple states, winning some and losing some.

But in at least one instance, Tesla has elevated a state-level challenge to a federal court. The case flowed out of a dispute in Michigan.

It may well die in the US District Court with jurisdiction. Or it could signal that Tesla has every intention of playing hardball until it gets an audience with the US Supreme Court.

The company's central premise—that the franchise laws are archaic contributors to a level of market inefficiency that limits consumer choice and convenience—may well find receptive ears on the nation's highest court.

All in all, I'm not trying to say the sky is falling when it comes to federal oversight and regulation.

I am, however, suggesting that the legacy of federal attention and interest in F&I practices, recalls, and franchise law challenges signals that these will be the three areas of increased regulatory risk and disruption for dealers in the immediate years ahead.

I tend to agree with the dealers who believe a Republican administration is much less likely to advance regulatory momentum to any of these areas.

But I also believe that once the federal government demonstrates a keen interest in an issue, it never really goes away.

8

DREAM HOMES AND DEALERSHIP DATA STREAMS

L et's imagine that you are building a dream home. You've got a secluded piece of property. It's near a lake. You purchased it through a friend of a friend. It's the property you've had in mind for years.

Your new home is the centerpiece of dinner conversations. You've spent several evenings with your significant other, wine, and an architect, sketching out the building plans.

One of your first priorities will be water. The property lies too far from the local municipal water supply to connect a line. The architect affirms that you'll need to dig a well.

The architect suggests two dominant well providers to consider for the job, saying that while they're more expensive, they've got capacity smaller operators might not deliver. The justification includes the package deals that include the well as well as the water and plumbing lines for your entire house.

You do your homework. It affirms the architect's guidance. Most home builders go with the larger, more well-established providers, even though they're more costly.

Construction goes mostly as planned. You, your significant other, and your family are pleased and proud as your dream house takes shape. Your evenings at the dinner table shift from discussions on the foundation and framing to the finishing touches that will truly make the house your home.

But here's where the trouble starts.

You learn, to your surprise, that your deal with Acme Incorporated, the company you chose for the well and plumbing, includes a few critical catches in the fine print.

The first catch is fixtures. You learn you have less flexibility to pick and choose the fixtures for your new home than you thought. In some cases, like the showerhead and faucet, you can only use Acme products. In other cases, like bathroom faucets and sinks, you can use third-party fixtures for the sink, but you have to buy the sink itself from Acme.

The second catch relates to surcharges. You determine that Acme's contract includes additional surcharges to attach any fixture, whether it comes from them or a third party, to the plumbing they've installed. Even worse, you find out the surcharges aren't one-time fees. The contract requires that as long as your fixtures attach to the Acme system, you pay an ongoing fee.

You go back to your Acme representative. You question the contract's fixture and surcharge provisions. How on earth is it OK for them to essentially force you to use their products and pay ongoing fees to access the water that you own the rights to access and use and is necessary for you to fully enjoy your new home?

The response, unfortunately, is not very satisfying.

The rep informs you that Acme's fixtures and surcharge conditions result from its efforts to ensure the integrity, purity, and security of your home's well water and plumbing system. Further, the rep tells you that, technically, you don't own the water once it flows through the well and water lines that serve your house.

This entire dream house scenario sounds a little preposterous, doesn't it?

Yet, it's not that much different than the situation many dealers face due to the policies and practices of the dominant dealer solutions providers who serve the automotive retail industry.

Think about it: The water in the dream home scenario is effectively the same as the data your dealership generates in the course of business every day. This data flows through your dealership, connecting with distinct systems in each dealership department. Some of these systems are part of a package deal with a single solutions provider; others come from separate, third-party providers.

The problem, of course, is that dealers too often pay surcharges as their data moves from one system to another—much like the fees Acme Incorporated charges to connect fixtures and ensure running water throughout the dream home.

The solutions providers say these surcharges are justified and necessary. They are intended to cover the costs of integrating these disparate systems and ensuring a protected, reliable flow of data.

I would disagree. These charges, in my view, sap dealership efficiency and profitability. The charges also slow the pace of technological innovation that could truly help dealers serve their customers in the manner they prefer.

DATA INTEGRATION FEES: A HIDDEN TAX OR JUSTIFIABLE EXPENSE?

Some industry observers have called the solutions providers' integration-related surcharges a hidden tax on dealers. They estimate the costs of the surcharges to be several thousand dollars for each dealer, depending on the number of users connected to the systems, as well as the volume of data that passes through the integrations.

For their part, the solutions providers typically cite the need for data security as the chief justification for the additional fees.

But my conversations and research suggest a few problems with this position: degree of risk, costs, level of protection, and hidden taxes and opportunity costs.

Degree of risk

At least one dealership information technology (IT) consultant questions whether the vast majority of data that flows through the various solutions really represents a security risk for dealers. The consultant says, "The bulk of the data in the dealership management system is not the type of stuff that hackers want: part numbers, repair history, accounting detail. Hackers want social security numbers, previous employers, existing payments amounts, credit card numbers, and credit history for a dealer's customers."

> **"The bulk of the data in the dealership management system is not the type of stuff that hackers want."**

The consultant's observation raises two key questions: Why are dealers paying extra to protect data that doesn't create an imminent threat? Second, shouldn't dealers have the right to determine the data that merits additional protection and security, rather than being told it's always necessary?

Over time, I believe these questions, and their answers, will be of critical interest to dealers.

Costs

As noted earlier, some estimate the costs of data integration and security amount to be several thousand dollars for individual dealers, depending on the amount of data, number of users, and other factors. Dealers don't necessarily see these costs on billing statements from solutions providers. They are often buried as pass-through costs.

I'm also told these costs can amount to highway robbery, given the prevailing market costs for firewalls and other data security measures. Even worse, these costs continue to rise, particularly as some solutions providers rely on the income to meet their profit and shareholder objectives.

Every time I ask dealers, or even solutions providers, what additional benefits these costs bring, I get a look that says, "C'mon, are you crazy?"

Level of protection

My research into dealership data security breaches affirms what other observers have found: More often than not, they result from bad behavior by dealership employees, rather than the breakdowns in the back-end mechanics of data exchange or extraction between dealership solutions.

You have to ask the question: If the solutions providers cite data certification and security as the chief justification for the charges and fees, exactly what kind of protections and recourse would dealers get if a data exchange–related security breach occurred?

I certainly hope that dealers will never face this question and, if they do, that they don't end up holding the short end of the stick.

Hidden taxes and opportunity costs

I'm somewhat surprised by dealer reactions when I discuss the costs of the hidden taxes that accompany DMS integrations.

Like the guy building his dream house, some are angry. They've canceled deals with solutions providers over the principle of paying money to access their own dealership data.

But most dealers, it seems, simply face the music. They begrudgingly pay what's required to run their businesses, even if it feels like a fleece job.

Part of the acceptance owes to a lack of transparency. The data security surcharges aren't always fully disclosed on billing statements. Some might even make the case that individual fees, in the context of the thousands of dollars dealers pay every month for IT solutions, don't amount to much.

I'd disagree. If you look beyond the hard costs dealers pay for these fees, there's an even larger consequence of the industry's pay-to-play state of dealership data access, integration, and management.

For example, a few months ago, a contact at a prominent venture capital company asked for my opinion about a new technology that would help dealers increase productivity and profits in their service departments.

To be candid, I was quite impressed by the vision of the entrepreneurial team. I thought their solution would have serious legs, particularly given the rise of margin compression in variable operations and the growing necessity for dealers to optimize customer pay work and retention.

But I asked a couple key questions: What plans did the team have in place to access the customer data that would be necessary for their solution to work? To what extent had they accounted for the surcharge costs they'd incur to access the data that would make the solution actually work?

Funny thing is, I was the first to ask the questions. This was a team of top-notch venture capitalists, with smart analysts accustomed to sizing up and uncovering risks in unfamiliar markets. Their efforts hadn't sniffed out the data integration issue or the associated costs. They'd assumed they'd just need the dealer's permission to access data—not negotiate with other solutions providers.

"We punted on the deal," my contact told me a couple weeks later. "We liked the product. But we didn't think it wise to invest several million dollars in a market with such steep barriers to entry."

Poof!

Just like that, an innovation that might have helped dealers provide a more technology-rich service experience went away. Now, it's possible the entrepreneurs might have found other investors, but to my knowledge they've turned their attention to building innovations that benefit other industries, where data access is less constricted and costly.

This is just one example. It's impossible to know how many other dealer-focused innovations have died on the vine as entrepreneurs discover the inherent costs and difficulties associated with connecting their solutions to dealership data.

Dealers themselves can likely think of one or two solutions that showed promise but ultimately failed due to the barriers they encountered trying to link their solutions to a particular DMS.

I'm hard-pressed to think of another industry that suffers from the inefficient flow of information, and the associated costs of lost opportunity and stifled innovation, as much as automotive retail.

There's no question in my mind that, in time, our industry will reach a breaking point. The current situation of pay-to-play data access won't be sustainable over the long haul.

I recall some years ago, dealers and industry observers once looked to Microsoft as a potentially disruptive force that could spur a less constricted and less costly flow of dealership data.

> **"I'm hard-pressed to think of another industry that suffers from the inefficient flow of information, and the associated costs of lost opportunity and stifled innovation, as much as automotive retail."**

I, for one, think such disruption would be a good thing—especially for the companies that increasingly rely on the data surcharges to sustain their legacy businesses.

In the end, a dealership may not be a dream house.

But every franchised store is a dream maker. It's the foundation on which the aspirations, future fortunes, and success of their owners and families are built.

I believe dealers deserve the opportunity to build these

dreams in a more unencumbered manner than they can achieve today—free of hidden data taxes and unnecessary charges. and free to apply these resources to more beneficial, productive, and profitable outcomes.

OK. The cat's out of the bag. Let's see how long it takes before someone catches it.

9

A KINDLY CALL FOR IMPROVED OEM PRODUCTION EFFICIENCY

I don't really know any dealers who are completely satisfied with the way their original equipment manufacturers (OEM) handle the production and allocation of new vehicles.

Some dealers love their product line but can't get enough of the right models and combinations. They know they'd sell more if they had them.

Other dealers are hungry for a better mix. They've got sedans coming out of their ears and simply don't have the crossovers, SUVs, or trucks today's buying public wants in ever-greater numbers.

On one level, you could forgive OEMs for missing the boat

on the current demand for larger vehicles given their years-long planning and production cycles. True, consumers have been moving away from sedans for years, but who knew that in 2016 you could buy gas for less than $2.00 a gallon?

Still, in light of all the requirements OEMs put on their dealer partners, it's fair to suggest that OEMs could become more efficient in aligning the vehicles they produce with the ones consumers actually want to buy. After all, it's the dealers who end up paying the ultimate price in slower-moving cars, higher incentives, and increased pressure on used vehicle values.

The level of product-to-demand inefficiency seems particularly acute this year—which has me worried what the future will look like when new vehicle demand eventually levels off and slows down.

> "It's far too common for dealers to have what might be considered dead stock on their lots. These vehicles have been there for longer than three months."

I see the effects of this inefficiency first hand as I discuss and evaluate inventory management shortcomings with dealers.

In new vehicles, it's far too common for dealers to have what might be considered dead stock on their lots. These vehicles have been there for longer than three months. Out of a two hundred-unit inventory, these slow-selling vehicles might account for as many as eighty to a hundred units. To be sure, this problem is worse for dealers who don't systematically optimize their factory orders for local supply and demand or efficiently manage their new vehicle merchandising and pricing against current market conditions.

Nonetheless, these vehicles don't all reflect less-than-optimal inventory management decisions at the dealership. Some are the direct result of factories producing vehicles the market doesn't really want and working their dealer networks to find a place to put them and get paid.

In used vehicles, the effects of the factory product-to-demand inefficiency are less direct and often manifest in long-term opportunity costs rather than short-term losses.

For example, used vehicle inventories at franchise dealerships are increasingly near new, a product of unprecedented numbers of off-lease vehicles, a shrinking share of new or used vehicle purchases that involve a trade-in, and factory programs that encourage service loaner, rental, and shuttle cars. I'm sure the parts department employees appreciate their pristine rides, but let's be honest: These cars should never really have counted as retail sales, and they're making things more difficult for used vehicle managers.

Add in the rise of off-lease vehicles, and you've got a slow, systematic consolidation of used vehicle inventories. By the end of 2016, 60 percent of dealers' used vehicle inventories were less than three years old. A few years ago, these vehicles accounted for closer to 45 percent of dealer inventories.

On one hand, it makes perfect sense to play to the near-new hand in used vehicles. These vehicles are certainly more abundant and, therefore, easier to acquire. These cars also help dealers meet factory retail and CPO sales targets. And, to the extent the models fit local market demand, they make sense for dealers to retail.

But on the other hand, the near-new vehicles cost more, and they expose dealers to a greater degree of risk, particularly as manufacturers apply bigger incentives to retail the same or similar new vehicles. Meanwhile, buyers want, but can't necessarily afford, these newer, higher-cost cars. Some of these buyers would fit right into a six- or seven-year-old car, but dealers don't have them in stock to sell.

To be sure, dealers ultimately choose the used vehicles to stock and retail, but there's only so much capital a dealer can, and should, invest in their inventories. If the factory's pushing a dealer to stock and sell more near-new vehicles to meet some type of incentive program goal, there's little doubt this pressure influences a dealer's inventory investment decisions.

In fairness to the factories, they have done a better job in recent years of striking a balance between supply and demand as they plan their production schedules. Inventory levels today may be higher than many dealers would prefer. But, overall, the imbalances are less steep compared to the days when it seemed like every dealer needed to lease extra space to accommodate the cars coming from the factory.

We should also recognize that factory vehicle planning and production across multiple model lines is no easy task. In addition to consumer preferences, factories must account for regulatory standards for emissions and fuel efficiency, economic factors like fuel prices, as well as their own desires for market share and profit as they determine production mix and volume. Typically, executives make these decisions years before a vehicle ever lands on a dealer's lot. We also know that, as these early-on decisions don't pan out, vehicle allocations to dealers become, to put it charitably, far less consistent and further removed from on-the-ground needs and realities.

These dynamics help explain the current product-to-demand inefficiency in today's new vehicle market. But they definitely don't excuse the problem.

Just as dealers must become more operationally and market-efficient in their businesses, factories must follow suit. I'm not qualified to speak to the intricacies of *how* OEMs become more efficient.

But, directionally speaking, it seems like factories could and should find a way to incorporate current consumer interests and market conditions into their vehicle planning and production schedules and subsequent allocations to dealers.

Such a shift would likely cause disruption at corporate headquarters. OEM organizations aren't exactly accustomed to changing the way they do business, much less making changes quickly.

I'm confident, however, that OEMs who move most quickly to strike a more efficient balance between production and consumer demand will fare better than those who resist the change. These OEMs will continue to chase short-term profits and miss the long-haul benefits of improved product-to-demand efficiency.

OEMs who choose this path will do their dealers a great service, consistently equipping them with the right inventory for their markets.

From there, it's up to the dealers.

And, as we all know, when dealers have the right inventory, they know how to compete, capture customers, sell more cars, and make more money. That seems like a pretty positive outcome any OEM would be willing (and wise) to embrace.

10

SHOULD YOU DO IT YOURSELF OR PAY SOMEONE ELSE?

There are a lot of things in life that, over time, no longer make sense. For many guys my age, changing the oil in your car or mowing your lawn fall into this bucket. At one time, both of these tasks made perfect sense. You had the time. You liked not paying someone else for the work. You might have even enjoyed getting your hands dirty and feeling the sense of accomplishment that comes from doing these jobs yourself.

But time passes. Life progresses. Your off-work hours become more precious. Other priorities, like work, family, exercise, or a hobby, take precedence. You may feel a loss of pride and purpose as you hire someone else to do work that, aside from your time constraints, you know you could do yourself. You might even still think you could do the job better than the person you pay to do it.

So goes the ever-present press for efficiency and productivity that marks business and life in the twenty-first century. At some point, we all question whether some job or task is worth our time and effort as we weigh the costs and benefits of doing it ourselves.

As market conditions continue to require dealers to achieve ever-higher levels of operational efficiencies, I believe there are at least two elements of dealership operations that, over time, may go the way of oil changes and lawn mowing.

USED VEHICLE RECONDITIONING

One of my colleagues relayed the story of how every summer weekend, he and his wife would end up bickering over his need to mow the lawn while she took care of their toddler son. The discussion never had a positive outcome. He'd get frustrated that she didn't understand his responsibility to keep the lawn tidy. She'd get frustrated that he seemed to miss the bigger picture—his desire to cut the grass was cutting out shared family time.

A similar standoff occurs in dealerships every day across the country.

The used vehicle manager bickers with the service director over the cost and time required to get vehicles reconditioned in a more efficient, profit-minded manner. The service director gets frustrated that the used vehicle manager doesn't respect his or her desire to serve paying customers first.

You can see evidence of this ongoing friction in average reconditioning times. For many dealers, it takes a week or more to get vehicles in or out of reconditioning and front-line ready. Dealers intuitively recognize that such delays cost them money; some studies suggest that each day a vehicle sits, not ready for retail sale, costs the dealer $85 in holding costs and lost front-end gross potential. If it takes seven days, that's nearly $600 a dealer loses to make roughly the same amount in service gross profit.

Unfortunately, many dealers do not analyze the costs of lost time in reconditioning this way. Their accounting doesn't recognize the lost time and opportunity cost. They count the gross profit they make in service as separate and distinct from the front-end gross they make when the car retails. They don't measure how delays in service sap the retail gross out of any car that sits too long. The lost productivity of technicians also goes unaddressed.

It's a lot like my colleague and his wife. They both understood that less shared family time represented some kind of a loss, but they never quantified it. Likewise, my colleague could point to money saved as evidence that he had, in fact, made a good decision from a household cash flow perspective.

This backdrop begs the question: If dealers can't resolve the reconditioning delays and inefficiencies, is it really worth the investment of effort, money, and time to continue doing this work?

Of course, dealers who *have* addressed and largely eliminated this inefficiency would say it absolutely makes financial sense to do the work in-house. Compared to their less reconditioning-efficient peers, they actually do enjoy the incremental benefits of increased gross profits in service and healthier front-end grosses. Cars get through the shop faster and sell more frequently when they're fresh and gross profits are ripe.

But these dealers will also say it takes a high degree of commitment and courage to facilitate a higher, more efficient level of collaboration and cooperation between the two departments. Their efforts include automatic repair order (RO) approvals, fixed fees for reconditioning work, in-depth tracking of reconditioning timelines, and pay plans that reward faster throughput.

Some dealers also effectively bypass the problem, creating stand-alone reconditioning centers that operate as separate businesses and focus solely on efficient, profitable reconditioning services.

I'm also aware that the mere suggestion of outsourcing reconditioning work runs counter to everything dealers have been taught about the benefits of operating a diversified business under one roof.

A comptroller for a Southeast store puts it this way, "Why would I pay someone else to make money when I can make the money myself? Besides that, there's risk. It's your name on the car, not the guy down the street who did the work."

At the same time, however, some larger dealer groups like Sonic Automotive are moving to an outsourced reconditioning model. They, too, had trouble resolving the age-old conflict between the used vehicle and service departments. For them, outsourcing offers a more cost-effective and time-efficient alternative. And the shift enables them to apply greater attention and resources to increasing customer pay work and retention.

Ultimately, I would encourage dealers to take a hard, honest look at their reconditioning processes and ask two key questions: Are we really making a sufficient return on the effort, resources, and time we invest in reconditioning, or are we actually hurting ourselves? If we're not fully optimized, do we have the courage and vision to fix the problem?

WHOLESALE SOURCING

Years ago, dealers who adopted the Velocity Method of Management in used vehicles realized a critical inefficiency. Their used vehicle managers were spending the bulk of their time outside the dealership, traveling to auctions to buy vehicles they needed to keep up their new-found pace of increased retail sales.

Like my colleague's wife, the dealers questioned whether the extended time out of the office was worth the effort, given the absence meant less time to work deals, oversee appraisers, approve reconditioning work, coach sales associates, price or reprice vehicles, and perform other tasks required to manage the used vehicle department.

In many stores, the dealers and used vehicle managers found a new way forward. They hired acquisition specialists to serve as buyers. Some split their time traveling to physical auctions and acquiring vehicles through online auctions. Others ditched physical auctions altogether, shifting their entire wholesale sourcing efforts to online channels.

Such changes brought positive results. Used vehicle managers were able to do a better job managing their departments. They had time to address too-slow turnarounds in reconditioning or inconsistencies among appraisers that resulted in booking fewer trade-ins than they could or should. They tightened up their pricing practices to help retail more used vehicles in less time.

On the acquisition front, the dealers and used vehicle managers also found they were acquiring better vehicles, thanks to the acquisition specialists' singular focus on acquiring cars that aligned with their target acquisition metrics and retail objectives. The acquisition specialists themselves also became highly adept at using available technology and tools to acquire cars more cost effectively and efficiently, which meant fewer instances of acquiring the wrong cars or purchasing them for too much money.

Today, there are a sizable number of dealers who have yet to rethink, much less reinvent, the way they source auction vehicles. They have yet to achieve the level of acquisition consistency and efficiency that have become standard operating procedures for their peers. As a result, they struggle to maintain a consistent supply of incoming inventory that represents the right cars, for the right money, for their dealerships. In turn, their pace of used vehicle retail sales and profitability suffers.

"There are a sizable number of dealers who have yet to rethink, much less reinvent, the way they source auction vehicles."

The problem for these dealers is that they have a lot of catching up to do. The dealers who underwent wholesale sourcing reinvention years ago are already heading in a different direction—one where they effectively outsource the acquisition of vehicles to a third party.

In some cases, the third party is a company that employs a team of buyers who work on behalf of their dealership clients and employ all of the available technologies and tools to efficiently deliver the vehicles their dealer clients need.

Auctions like Manheim have begun offering this type of broker-style service in earnest in recent months. Likewise, there are smaller companies pitching dealers on the idea that they can do the job of acquiring vehicles for less cost, less hassle, and less risk than if the dealers did the job themselves.

At the same time, there are efforts underway to achieve even greater levels of wholesale sourcing efficiencies by using technology to essentially automate the entire process. I'm involved in some of these efforts with Cox Automotive.

The high-level vision behind these efforts is that ever-smarter technologies can do the job of finding, assessing, and purchasing auction vehicles as good as, if not better than, the buyers working the physical sales and online channels today.

It's not inconceivable to imagine a day, in the not-too-distant future, where used vehicle managers or acquisition specialists can simply choose to approve an automated purchase and delivery of auction vehicles to their dealerships. These vehicles would essentially show up, and, depending on a dealer's preference to handle vehicle reconditioning in-house or outsource the work, they could be totally front-line ready right away.

Skeptics might think this future state is impossible to deliver. What if the system purchases the wrong cars, or the right cars arrive in poorer condition than expected? How can a tool possibly replace the "eyes, ears, and nose" that are necessary to assess a vehicle's retail potential?

These are valid questions. But, if you think about them, they are essentially the same questions dealers asked prior to purchasing auction vehicles, sight- and sniff-unseen, through online channels. They are the questions that have given rise to no-risk, buy-back options auction providers now offer dealers who prefer online auction purchases.

The overall point here is that wholesale sourcing is undergoing an efficiency- and technology-driven evolution. It is moving to a model where outsourced, technology-enabled services stand to provide dealers even higher levels of acquisition consistency and efficiency, both in terms of cost and time, than they can achieve today on their own.

In the months and years ahead, auction purchases will become another area that will force dealers to ask the question my colleague's wife posed to him: "Are you really better off doing this job yourself?"

I should note that my colleague and his wife are much happier these days. So is their son. And their lawn looks great.

"We spent last Saturday on a day-long hike—something I never thought we'd have time to do," my colleague says. "It was great . . . but then we got home. My wife looked at the stuff in the corner of the garage. Do you know anyone who needs a lawn mower?"

11

A TAXING PROBLEM THAT GOES UNADDRESSED IN USED VEHICLES

D ealers love packs and retail reconditioning fees. But I would submit that these long-standing practices, in today's more margin-compressed and transparent used vehicle environment, no longer provide the business benefits that once justified their existence.

I'll even go a step further: Overly high packs and retail reconditioning rates amount to nothing more than a tax on your used vehicles—one that does more damage than good. Even worse, the damage often goes unaddressed and unnoticed by dealers.

Now, hang on. You're probably thinking *WTF? Packs and retail reconditioning rates absolutely* do not *amount to a tax on my used vehicles. They make good business sense, and, besides, it's my right as a dealer to charge them.*

But let's take a moment to consider the definition of a *tax*. A tax is a charge or cost added to a good or service that is not offset by an equal or greater value than the amount of the tax itself. Further, taxes, by definition, increase the cost of doing business and, as a result, slow the pace of commerce.

Now, let's use this definition to evaluate whether packs and retail reconditioning rates, in today's market, could be considered a tax.

We'll start with packs.

PACKS

Historically, packs came about in an era when dealers worked from cost up in used vehicles. Dealers sometimes wouldn't admit this is how they ran their used vehicle department. But the day-to-day practice of acquiring cars, and applying standard markups and packs, suggests otherwise.

Packs primarily served to reduce the amount of commissionable gross profit paid to managers and sales teams. Dealers also used packs to create a fund, or pool of money, that could be used to offset unexpected repairs to vehicles and wholesale losses. In some cases, dealers used pack-generated funds to pay for customer loyalty-type programs, such as lifetime oil changes and limited warranties.

In my day as a dealer, it was pretty common for packs to run about $1,000 per car. Like most dealers I knew, we used the pack to cover unanticipated fixes to vehicles we'd just sold. I also used the money to pay for employee bonuses, facility repairs and upgrades, and, at times, to pad my bank account.

But, in today's market, dealers no longer work from cost up.

They have come to understand that in today's Internet-driven age of pricing transparency, a retail-back strategy is more important and relevant. In practice, this strategy finds dealers assessing the likely retail asking prices for a vehicle to determine how much they should pay to acquire it.

The retail-back strategy effectively eliminates the equal-or-greater-value offset to commissionable gross that originally justified packs as something other than a tax. The sky is no longer the limit when it comes to front-end gross profit, which undercuts the efficacy of a pack.

At the same time, there are fewer mechanical surprises with today's vehicles, and they're often less costly than they used to be. As such, the justification that packs provide the offset of peace of mind to cushion the cost of things like unexpected repairs loses its relevance.

Dealers could make a case that a pack that funds customer loyalty programs would not be a tax. If this is true, the pack must provide an amount of equal or greater value to offset the charge. The test: If you charge $1,000 per pack and the true cost of your loyalty program is $300, the $700 difference is, by definition, a tax.

I would also add that, across the country, dealers who have adopted the retail-back approach have cut, if not eliminated altogether, the packs they once charged. A $1,000 pack is no longer the de facto norm in every market. It's far more common to see dealers charge packs of $400 or less—a reflection, I believe, that dealers understand higher-dollar packs are problematic in today's margin-compressed environment.

> **"Across the country, dealers who have adopted the retail-back approach have cut, if not eliminated altogether, the packs they once charged."**

Let's now turn our attention to retail reconditioning fees and why, in today's market, these add-on costs function like a tax.

RETAIL RECONDITIONING FEES

To be sure, charging retail reconditioning fees is *not* as tax-problematic as adding a high-dollar pack to a used vehicle. No one questions whether reconditioning work adds value to a vehicle. Dealers can and should expect to profit from providing this service to their vehicles and future buyers.

The issue is whether the amount you charge adds an equal or greater value for the work performed.

Under this definition, if a dealer charges retail reconditioning labor and parts fees of $800, but the market value of the work is $400, the remaining $400 amounts to a tax that elevates the gross profit of the service department while taxing the vehicles with additional cost.

Further, when you combine a high-dollar pack with retail reconditioning fees, bad things start to happen in the used vehicle department—things that, unfortunately, many dealers miss or overlook.

HOW HIGH-DOLLAR PACKS AND RETAIL RECONDITIONING RATES TAX USED VEHICLE PERFORMANCE

I see the damaging effects of packs and retail reconditioning fees every day. These effects usually manifest in three ways.

1. A less than consistent and steady supply of incoming inventory

There are many dealers who could, and should, be selling more used vehicles, but they aren't able to effectively restock their lots.

If you dig a little deeper, you'll see buyers coming home empty-handed from auctions, low win rates for vehicles at online auctions, and too many trade-in opportunities that fell apart. These problems are far more pronounced at dealerships that charge more than a $400 pack and retail rates for reconditioning. Why? Because desk managers and buyers account for these add-on costs as they make acquisition decisions.

Time and time again, dealers will say, "Not my store. My desk managers and buyers ignore the pack or reconditioning fees."

But the on-the-ground reality is far different than these perceptions. These add-on costs influence every decision, whether the dealer wants to believe it or not.

Put yourself in the appraiser's or buyer's shoes for a moment.

In today's more margin-compressed environment, it's nearly impossible to add a $1,000 pack and retail reconditioning fees to the cost of a vehicle and expect a satisfactory gross profit. To be sure, you'll get lucky with some cars. But the market doesn't produce enough of them to keep your retail sales going at full throttle.

If you're the desk manager or buyer, you have one of two choices.

First, you can account for the cost of the pack and retail reconditioning fees as you acquire the car. You know the vehicle has a compromised front-end gross profit potential, and you know you're likely to catch grief for acquiring yet another low-grossing unit.

Your second choice isn't much better. You can simply pass on the car. "We couldn't get that deal done" or "The cars weren't there for us today" become repeated excuses. Pretty soon, the dealer's going to realize you don't have enough inventory and will lay down the law.

Either scenario suggests that desk managers and buyers are hobbled by high-dollar packs and retail reconditioning fees. They are taking full account of these add-on costs, to the detriment of every dealership where these costs get charged to every vehicle.

You can pretty much bet that dealers are essentially clueless about this problem. They may intuitively sense that they could be selling more cars if they had more inventory, but they don't realize the root cause of their inventory shortfall.

2. Less-than-optimal profitability and volume

I recently compared the used vehicle performance of two similarly sized and geographically located dealers. One dealer charged a $250 pack and internal reconditioning fees, the other a $1,000 pack and retail reconditioning fees.

The analysis included a rundown of each dealer's Cost-to-Market metric for their inventories. The dealer who charged a $250 pack and internal reconditioning fees had an 84 percent Cost to Market, which meant an average 16 percent profit margin spread between the cost required to acquire the unit and its average retail asking price.

The other dealer, who charged a $1,000 pack and retail reconditioning fees, had a 90 percent Cost to Market—a margin spread that's 6 percent less than the competing dealer. The disparity translated to about a $500 difference in the front-end gross profit average each dealer reported.

In addition, the dealer with the $250 pack sold nearly twice as many cars from an inventory roughly half the size of the $1,000-pack dealer.

Some dealers might question how this higher sales velocity is even possible. But the answer is pretty obvious: The dealer with the $250 pack and internal reconditioning rates is setting up his used vehicle manager and sales team to make money and succeed. His team members know they'll be rewarded for working hard to retail vehicles. Their commissionable gross isn't crimped by the dealer's decision to restrict each vehicle's profit potential. They feel good about going to work every day.

By contrast, the dealer with the $1,000 pack and retail reconditioning fees had a problem. His managers complained that they were forced to report too many low- or no-gross deals. They couldn't keep sales associates on the payroll, and at least one manager admitted he was thinking about working somewhere else. Who wants to work for a place where everything you do seems to produce a negative result?

I haven't done a formal study, but I suspect there's a direct correlation between the size of a turnover problem in a dealership and the size of the charges for a pack and reconditioning fees.

3. Inventory age problems

I was also curious to see how the packs and retail reconditioning fees might affect each dealer's ability to retail used vehicles quickly and minimize the risk of aging units.

My analysis showed that the dealer who charged a $250 pack and internal reconditioning fees retailed 65 percent of his inventory in less than thirty days and had only 7 percent older than sixty days. The dealer with the $1,000 pack and retail reconditioning fees sold 40 percent in thirty days and had 33 percent older than sixty days.

These insights made me wonder how the dealers were pricing their vehicles and whether the size of the pack made any difference.

The results weren't surprising: Out of the gate, the dealer with the $1,000 pack and retail reconditioning fees consistently priced his inventory well above the market—a symptom of a manager hoping to make gross on the

> **"I suspect there's a direct correlation between the size of a turnover problem in a dealership and the size of the charges for a pack and reconditioning fees."**

car. I also noted less-frequent, and larger, price reductions as vehicles aged.

By contrast, the dealer with the $250 pack and internal reconditioning fees priced his inventory at or slightly above the market from day one—the set-up that drives the ability to sell more cars while they're fresh. Similarly, the dealer's subsequent price reductions were more frequent and smaller in nature compared to the other dealer.

When I plotted the pricing patterns on a graph, one dealer's price slope looked like a bunny hill, while the other looked like a black diamond ski slope.

As I noted above, I see these damaging effects of high-dollar packs and retail reconditioning fees all the time. The worst part is that dealers are often unaware of the damage their decisions to tax their vehicles creates for their used vehicle department performance and profitability.

Perhaps the best part of the pack and retail reconditioning fee problem is how quickly it can go away, once a dealer decides the time is right.

"That was us a few years ago," says the dealer who charged the $250 pack and internal reconditioning fees in the analysis above. "We realized that we'd sell more cars, and make more money, if we scaled back our pack and reconditioning costs, which were slowing us down. It turned out to be a good decision. Our dealership's net profitability keeps getting better."

Such sentiments, and the disparities in performance and profitability I see between dealers who have reduced packs and reconditioning fees and those who haven't, lead me to my belief that dealers should at least revisit, if not rethink entirely, the way they levy these charges at their dealerships.

Perhaps these paraphrased words from Winston Churchill will help dealers realize their own tax problems in used vehicles: I contend that for a dealership to try to tax itself into prosperity is like a man standing in a bucket and trying to lift himself up by the handle.

12

A CALL FOR INVESTMENT-MINDED INVENTORY MANAGEMENT

I f I needed investment advice, I probably wouldn't go to a car dealer or a used vehicle manager. To be sure, I've come to respect dealers and used vehicle managers for their savvy and skills in retailing used vehicles. But I've found their actions and instincts as managers of investments in used vehicles leave a lot to be desired.

I say this due to the persistence and prevalence of aged used vehicle inventory on dealer lots across the country. By and large, these aged units are the cumulative result of bad investment decisions that, too often, could have been avoided.

Given the prevalence of these problematic vehicles, you have to ask two questions: Why do aged vehicles continue to be such a problem? And, what can be done to reduce, if not eliminate, the burden these aged cars create on a dealer's used vehicle inventory investment?

In this chapter, I'll do my best to answer these important questions.

HOW HISTORY AND HOPE CAUSE AGING PROBLEMS

Ever since the earliest days of the used vehicle business, dealers have understood that time matters. They know that used vehicles depreciate and that, over time, an aging unit loses its ability to drive front-end gross profit and deliver a sufficient return on investment (ROI).

Of course, dealers have differing opinions about *how much* time a vehicle deserves to stay in their inventory until it's become a burden. In my day as a dealer, you were typically either a 90-day or 120-day dealer. When a car crossed those timelines on your calendar, you knew you had to do something, whether it was a significant price reduction or wholesaling the unit.

But even those calendar milestones weren't all that meaningful. You still had a fair number of 150-, 180-, and 200-day-old cars in inventory.

If you ask dealers to explain what happened to these vehicles, they'd often share a similar story: The car's out of the money and they are hoping, or, in some cases, believing, that a buyer will come along who doesn't know any better.

Now, if you're like me, the last thing you want your personal finance investment manager to tell you is that we're hoping for a certain outcome. Hope suggests the investment manager doesn't have the market data or knowledge that builds confidence and indicates my investment is in capable hands. I might even start shopping around for someone else.

Nonetheless, I will concede that hope wasn't a completely unreasonable strategy back in the day for dealers. This was the "ass for every seat" era. Dealers had the upper hand. Buyers had to come to us to find their next vehicle. They didn't really know what any used vehicle was worth until we told them.

Those were the glory days in used vehicles. We could reasonably expect to put a retail-worthy vehicle on our front line, and someone would show up to buy it. Even better, if we had an aged unit, the market's inefficiency and lack of transparency gave us the ability to convince buyers that our out-of-the-money car, and asking price, was exactly the right choice for their next vehicle.

But when's the last time you heard anyone say "There's an ass for every seat," except in reference to the way things used to be?

Therein lies the problem. Hope is no longer a reasonable strategy in today's market. If your aged vehicle is the wrong car, or it's out of the money, buyers know it. That's why the car hasn't sold in the first place.

Hope also becomes highly irrelevant when you consider that dealers and used vehicle managers now have the ability to be more investment minded, given the prevalence of technology and tools that help you determine exactly how a vehicle will perform at retail. With such market insights in hand, there's really no longer any reason why hope should be a part of any used vehicle decision. Today, you really can tell if a used vehicle represents a poor investment decision from day one.

"Hope is no longer a reasonable strategy in today's market."

Here again, you have to ask why dealers and used vehicle managers don't take the first opportunity to get out of these vehicles. That's what investment managers would do. They understand that your first opportunity to exit is most often your best opportunity.

But history and tradition make it difficult for dealers and used vehicle managers to think this way.

As used vehicle retailers, we've been taught that losses and low grosses are bad and should be avoided. Hence, it's OK to hang on to a margin-challenged vehicle and hope for a better result.

Similarly, we've been conditioned to mind the age of our used vehicle inventories. If our effective hard stop on the retail life of a used vehicle is forty-five, sixty, or ninety days, what's the problem with putting a car out there in the hope of getting lucky?

Years ago, tracking a vehicle's age across the calendar made sense. We didn't really have any other metric by which to measure a vehicle's relative investment potential as a retail unit.

But compared to the technology-driven market insights dealers and used vehicle managers have at their disposal today, the calendar looks more like a sundial than a useful gauge of whether we're properly managing the quality of our investments in used vehicles.

It is for all these reasons that I wouldn't entrust most dealers and used vehicle managers to serve as stewards of my money. Their instincts as retailers tend to trump their ability to act and think like the investment managers they really should be. The persistence of overage inventory stands as testimony to a general lack of investment discipline and sophistication in dealerships across the country.

Which brings us to the second question—what can be done to help dealers and used vehicle managers become more astute managers of the money they invest in used vehicles and reduce the proliferation of aged cars in inventory?

The answer to this persistent problem lies, I believe, in two new best practices I'd like to propose for the industry.

1. Manage investment quality, not inventory age

As I've tried to note above, managing inventory age leads to less-than-optimal outcomes—a fall-back reliance on the hope that you'll get lucky with profit-troubled vehicles and the persistent press of aged inventory on your used vehicle performance and profitability.

But the real problem is that age is the wrong metric to manage—it's the money, or the quality of your investment in each used vehicle, that really matters.

Think about it: A vehicle that, for whatever reason, isn't blessed with the ability to deliver a satisfactory and sufficient margin contribution from day one usually doesn't get any better by days five, ten, fifteen, or twenty.

Dealers and used vehicle managers generally understand that a distressed used vehicle will only get worse. But their retail instincts and traditional training get in the way of making decisions from an investment perspective.

> **"Dealers and used vehicle managers find it difficult to view the early signs of a poor investment in a used vehicle as an opportunity."**

Unlike investment managers, dealers and used vehicle managers find it difficult to view the early signs of a poor investment in a used vehicle as an opportunity—a cue or curtain call to redeploy their capital into another car that offers greater potential to make a satisfactory and sufficient return.

The key, of course, is knowing how to assess a vehicle's investment health right away to avoid making a bad or questionable investment, which will only get worse over time.

The assessment should cover these elements:

- **An eyes-on assessment of a vehicle.** This physical assessment of every car should aim to answer a simple question: Is this vehicle likely to excite a prospective buyer or is it a so-so unit or even worse?

- **The vehicle's Cost-to-Market ratio.** Given your acquisition cost, as well as costs for a pack, reconditioning, transportation, and so on, how close is your total investment to your average retail market price? The answer to this question determines the likely front-end gross profit the vehicle might achieve and is a key indicator of whether it will deliver a sufficient ROI.

- **The vehicle's Market Days Supply.** This metric gives you a sense of the supply and demand for a specific vehicle and how fast the unit will retail. In general, the lower a vehicle's Market Days Supply, the greater the likelihood that it will sell quickly and help you maximize your ROI.

On a day-to-day basis, here's how this assessment plays out.

Let's say you have two vehicles you're considering to acquire. The first looks very sharp. After your pack and reconditioning, you own it at an 84 percent Cost-to-Market ratio, which gives you a respectable 16 percent spread between your investment and its prevailing retail price. The Market Days Supply is sixty days, which suggests a relatively high level of demand in relation to supply.

The second vehicle is more plain, with less likely shopper appeal. After your pack and reconditioning, you own it for an amount very close to its average retail asking price. The Market Days Supply is ninety-three days, which suggests it'll take some time to retail.

The investment quality of the two vehicles should be readily apparent. The first car represents a decent risk and offers the prospect of a sufficient ROI. The second car has all the makings of a soon-to-be-aged unit if you choose to retail it.

You'll notice that, in this exercise, which I suggest dealers and used vehicle managers perform with every prospective acquisition at day one, the age of the vehicle isn't even mentioned. That's because age is irrelevant when you focus on the quality of your investment in each used vehicle.

Dealers will often complain that today's era of price transparency and technology-aided decisions have ruined the car business. I beg to differ. I regard the ability to determine a vehicle's investment quality from day one as a blessing that every prior generation of dealers and used vehicle managers would have wished they had in hand.

2. Set a hard cap on your inventory investment

I recognize that old habits are awfully hard to break. Whether it's drinking, smoking, or overeating, it's tough to retrain your body and mind that, from now on, things will truly be different.

The same is true for dealers and used vehicle managers as they make the transition from being retailers to being more financially astute managers of their used vehicle investments. Unfortunately, this transition will require some tough love for dealers and used vehicle managers to break themselves from relying on hope and inventory age as guiding, operational principles.

The solution, I believe, is to create an environment that not only encourages but also requires investment management discipline.

That's why I propose that every dealer institute a hard cap or limit on their used vehicle inventory investment. Managers have x dollars to spend and manage in a given year, and that's it.

In effect, the hard cap or limit on your inventory investment would function like a household budget. You only have x dollars at your disposal, which requires that you make the best possible use of the money.

If you ask dealers and used vehicle managers for their total used vehicle investment, you'll typically get ballpark figures that range between $500,000 and $1.5 million.

For the most part, dealers don't really track their total inventory investment. They have a general sense of how much money they've got tied up in inventory. They may also know that the total investment amount tends to fluctuate—shifts they often attribute to changes in market conditions.

But I don't think market conditions cause the fluctuations as much as dealers think. I would bet that much, if not all, of the investment flux owes to the aged cars and losses that result from an overreliance on hope on the part of managers.

It's almost like used vehicle managers are trust fund babies. If they make a bad financial decision, they just tap the trust for more money. They don't face real consequences for their less-than-astute decisions. Their access to additional funds effectively covers up their transgressions.

That's why I've begun advocating for a hard cap or limit on each dealer's inventory investment.

Without this gate, used vehicle managers have an open checkbook. There's no structural impediment that forces them to become more disciplined, investment minded, and market smart as they acquire, merchandise, price, and retail their used vehicles.

The end result would be nothing but a positive for used vehicle managers and their dealers. The cap would force both to get past hope and inventory age and focus their attention on what really matters—maximizing the return on investment in every used vehicle.

I hope that someday, I'll see signs that dealers and used vehicle managers are operating like financially astute investment managers. I'll see fewer aged vehicles in dealers' used vehicle inventories across the country. I'll see better ROI metrics for their current (and capped) inventory investments.

Maybe then, I'll feel more confident about calling one of them for investment advice.

13

THE OPERATIONAL EFFICIENCY IMPERATIVE FOR DEALERS

Take a moment and ponder these questions: How many of your former competitors have sold out to other dealers in recent years? How many of those deals went to a local competitor? How many involved you as the buyer?

I hate to say it, but I believe dealers who affirmatively answered the last question have a better likelihood of being in business in the not-too-distant future than those who've simply watched the buy/sell activity from the sidelines.

I say this because, more and more, the car business is becoming a game where size, scale, and operational efficiencies are the necessary ingredients for long-term profitability, relevance, and viability.

You can see this reality in the buy/sell activity of recent years.

The Banks Report notes that nearly 1,350 dealerships changed hands between 2013 and 2016—a record-setting pace for the industry. Through this period, the number of dealership rooftops has remained largely stable, around 18,000, while the number of dealership owners has shrunk to about 8,000.

Analysts expect consolidation to continue over the next decade. By 2025, some predict we'll have 16,500 dealerships, with just 6,500 owners, in an environment where profit margins continue to compress.

As consolidation continues, it's not unreasonable to think that the top one hundred megadealers, who currently own about 17 percent of dealership rooftops and command a similar share of new and used vehicle sales, could account for 25 percent or more of the retail market—with even higher concentration and control in specific geographic regions.

This outlook suggests that virtually every dealer, in every market, will soon be competing against someone bigger—someone whose size and scale could be efficiently and properly applied, giving them an inherent, operationally driven, competitive, and financial advantage.

Some advantages are evident already. Efficiency-minded dealer groups are using their economies of scale to renegotiate big-ticket costs like healthcare benefits, DMS fees, and insurance. In some cases, they might now pay only a third of the costs smaller dealers incur, on a same-store basis, for similar goods and services. In today's era of compressed margins, where even nickels and dimes matter, this more-efficient cost structure automatically creates competitive opportunity.

I don't know about you, but when I was a dealer, I appreciated the fact that, even if I lost out to a competitor, I felt like I had an equal chance to win one the next day. The other dealer was often a lot like me—a single- or dual-point, family-owned operation that sold about the same number of cars, made about the same amount of money, and ran things more or less the same way.

Instead, we appear to be entering an era where a growing number of dealers are in position to use their economies of scale to consistently stock better new and used vehicles, sell and service them at lower prices and margins, and make more money—at the expense of their less-efficient, smaller-scale competition.

The takeaway here isn't that every dealer had better be on the acquisition trail, or else. Not at all. In fact, I question whether the inefficiencies that are common in many dealerships today will spell trouble for dealers who have made growth through acquisition a primary strategy.

In fact, for these dealers, what I call the *efficiency imperative* will be even more critical if they expect to realize the returns they desire from their acquisition investments. As I've noted

> "Today's market is one where simply owning more stores, and selling and servicing more cars, won't be enough to remain relevant and viable as retailers."

in earlier chapters, today's market is one where simply own-ing more stores, and selling and servicing more cars, won't be enough to remain relevant and viable as retailers.

What is the efficiency imperative?

It's really a commitment and conviction to aggressively limit, if not eliminate, the long-standing operational inefficiencies that have gone unaddressed for far too long by far too many dealers. Broadly speaking, these inefficiencies fall into the fol-lowing categories.

INVENTORY INEFFICIENCY

A key litmus test for inventory inefficiency rests on two factors—what percentage of your new and used vehicles do you sell within thirty days, and what percentage of your inventory is more than forty-five days old (used) and ninety days old (new).

In used vehicles, dealers should strive to retail at least 55 percent of their inventory in less than thirty days, and the remainder within forty-five days. These benchmarks aren't easy to achieve, but doing so helps dealers focus their efforts on acquiring the right vehicles, reconditioning them quickly, pric-ing them right, and retailing them before market volatility and depreciation sap their return on investment potential.

In new vehicles, dealers should strive to retail 50 percent of their inventory in less than thirty days and retail the rest within ninety days, allowing no more than 10 percent of all new vehicles to linger past the three-month mark. These standards effectively force dealers to adopt more disciplined and market-focused stocking, pricing, and dealer trade decisions to boost their sales velocity and overall inventory and investment efficiency.

The inventory efficiency imperative will be especially critical for smaller dealers, who lack the clout and scale of their larger, multi-rooftop competitors. The larger dealers have greater ability to shift inventory to different dealerships to meet market demand and spread inventory costs across more balance sheets.

But this scale advantage only goes so far. Why? Because we all know that having the right new or used vehicle, with the correct color, equipment, trim, and features and a competitive price, is increasingly the primary factor that determines whether a buyer chooses to give you the first shot at their business. Therein lies an efficiency advantage that's up for grabs by anyone.

CUSTOMER INEFFICIENCY

For years, industry experts have been telling dealers that today's customers desire two things more than anything else—a higher level of pricing and process transparency and less time required in the showroom.

Yet if you look at the way dealers typically market their vehicles and services online, and handle them in the showroom, it's quite clear that many dealers still do not embrace these expectations, creating an inefficiency that makes it more difficult to earn customers' trust and their business.

As we discussed in an earlier chapter, addressing this inefficiency starts online. Are you truly facilitating the parts of the sales process and transaction that a growing number of customers want to complete online, or do you view online engagements as simply a way to generate a lead and make an appointment? Does your showroom process effectively pick up from where you and the customer left things online, or do you require them to effectively start from square one when they meet your sales associate?

These are the questions that, as dealers answer them, yield the level of customer efficiency that cements purchase intentions and trust and brings a greater share of business to your door.

MARKETING INEFFICIENCY

For as long as I can remember, NADA has pegged dealers' average cost of marketing per new vehicle retailed at roughly $600. One would think that in today's retail environment, where buyers effectively sell themselves as they research new and used vehicles online, this cost would be declining on a year-over-year basis.

But it isn't, which begs me to ask why? As I've sought to answer the question, I've become convinced that force of habit and ineffective execution are the chief culprits behind a per-car marketing cost that could, and should, be significantly lower.

Industry data suggests that dealers' marketing budgets split roughly 75/25, with 75 percent spent in traditional channels like newspapers, radio, and TV and the remaining 25 percent spent in digital media. To me, this allocation seems out of step with consumers, who increasingly look online to research cars, validate their needs, and pick a dealer.

Some digitally minded dealers have reversed the marketing spend, putting a significant majority of their investments online. Others have gone further, dumping traditional advertising altogether, adopting an all-digital marketing strategy.

Both approaches seem far more cost-effective and relevant to reach and engage today's buyers and to reduce the $600 per car cost.

I'm aware of several all-digital dealers who say their current marketing cost per vehicle is less than $200 per car, and they believe less than $100 is achievable, even as they reach and serve more customers. The key: Fully integrating all of their online marketing efforts and ensuring they consistently convey their customer-friendly message of transaction transparency and speed.

The good news? These marketing efficiency improvements, and the profit improvements they bring to the bottom line, are available to every dealer, regardless of the size and scope of their operations.

TECHNOLOGY INEFFICIENCY

I see signs of this inefficiency every day in my conversations with dealers. There's always someone, it seems, who isn't using a dealer's existing technology and tools to their fullest potential—whether it's the sales associate updating (or checking) your customer relationship management (CRM) system to capture a customer's information or gain insights on their preferences; a used vehicle manager or appraiser entering all the appropriate information in your inventory management system to properly appraise and price vehicles; a general manager who isn't tracking key performance indicators (KPIs) that virtually every dealership software solution offers to help you make smarter operational decisions and avoid the same mistakes; a service advisor who refuses to use a tablet-based repair order (RO) writing tool.

To be sure, the technical inefficiencies could be traced to poor hiring, process, and training issues. Whatever the root cause, the end results are less-than-satisfactory levels of productivity, proficiency, and profitability for your dealership. The upshot: If you hope to compete effectively against bigger players and peers, and meet your investment return objectives for your dealership in years to come, technical efficiency and proficiency will become paramount.

HUMAN CAPITAL INEFFICIENCY

Given the earlier chapter on human capital optimization, I won't dwell much on this topic here. But it must be made clear that dealers cannot allow the turnstile-like state of employee hiring and retention to continue if they aspire to remain a viable business.

This opportunity is even more pronounced for smaller dealers, who lack the size and scale to offer a wide variety of career path options that many younger applicants want to see—and larger groups increasingly offer.

Most important, tomorrow's hires will perform and produce to the extent that you give them the confidence, resources, sense of security, and training they need to call your dealership their career home.

CHANGE INEFFICIENCY

If there's one area of the car business where smaller dealers might be best suited to compete against larger dealers, it would be the former's inherent, size-driven ability to adapt and change more quickly.

Think of David and Goliath. For all intents and purposes, David shouldn't have stood a chance against the much-larger Goliath. But David was a little more cunning and a little faster on his feet. In the end, he triumphed.

> **"Smaller dealers have what might be called a *David advantage* when it comes to embracing and adapting to change."**

Smaller dealers have what might be called a *David advantage* when it comes to embracing and adapting to change. By their nature, smaller dealers can adjust and change faster than larger dealer groups. But the key test will be whether they choose to do so. In my view, the advantage and opportunity will go to dealers, regardless of size, who become more change efficient. They will have the least trouble adapting to change, particularly as the pace of change gains even more momentum.

In the end, I think dealers should regard the efficiency imperative as the price of entry to a brighter future. Today, it's not fully clear what the future dealer will really look like. Some predict a mix of big stores and satellite locations, standalone service facilities, e-enabled showrooms without any physical cars, and, yes, factory-mandated tile schemes.

Whatever the case, it seems clear to me that any dealer who aspires to be part of the evolution must get there first—which won't happen if you're limping along, hampered by your own inefficiencies.

14

A KODAK MOMENT FOR DEALERS AND OUR INDUSTRY?

"**W**hat business are you in?"

If you asked that question to one hundred dealers, the vast majority would say, "I'm in the business of selling cars."

A smaller segment would say, "I'm in the business of selling and servicing cars."

Few, if any, however, would say, "I'm in the transportation business."

To me, these responses suggest a potential problem as two big trends converge on automotive retail—the rise of ride-sharing services and the advent of self-driving cars.

Even as I write, original equipment manufacturers (OEM)

like Ford are inking deals with Uber to put driverless cars on highways and streets across America. Google's in the game, as are dozens of other companies that seek to disrupt the long-standing natural order of how Americans buy, own, and use automobiles.

Every week, it seems, there's a news story highlighting a fresh partnership or plan by some company to capitalize on ride-sharing and self-driving cars. I've found it next to impossible to keep up with who's doing what as these trends converge.

But here's what you don't see in the coverage: the impact and implications of ride-sharing services and self-driving cars for dealers. To me, the absence of any dealer-related discussion amounts to a deafening and scary silence.

Not long ago, I was invited to participate in an industry podcast to discuss the future of franchised dealerships and the role they would play as ride-sharing and self-driving cars became more ubiquitous. The podcast's central premise: a debate or discussion about a new dealership business model, where dealers would provide transportation services, in addition to servicing vehicles.

I thought long and hard about this vision for dealerships. And the more I thought about it, the less plausible it seemed.

Doesn't the future business model of dealership-as-a-transportation-and-service-facilitator pretty much describe every rental car facility at airports across America? Wouldn't the current network of largely privately held dealerships lack the efficiency and scale to replace the existing owners of large vehicle fleets and centralized service centers?

Ultimately, I declined the invitation. I didn't feel enlightened or informed enough on the subject to be a worthy contributor. I also feared that my perspective, as a long-time advocate for dealers who now worries about their future prosperity and relevance, would not be constructive or instructive for the conversation.

But I can't hold my tongue any longer. Someone has to speak up, if for nothing else to publicly offer a cautionary look at the reasons why the convergence of ride-sharing services and self-driving vehicles casts a dark, ominous cloud over the future of automotive retailing.

RIDE-SHARING AS THE NEXT EVOLUTION OF VEHICLE OWNERSHIP AND USE

About a hundred years ago, automobile manufacturers realized they had a problem.

It wasn't that the vehicles they produced were unpopular. In fact, demand often outstripped supply back in those days—a seemingly perfect situation for factory owners like Henry Ford to continue to scale their fast-growing businesses.

The problem proved to be affordability. The average family wasn't making enough back then to amass the lump sum payment needed to purchase an automobile.

General Motors is credited as the first manufacturer to begin offering what we now know as financing to help consumers afford the vehicles they desired—and fuel even faster growth in vehicle production and profits for manufacturers. At the time, Henry Ford reportedly scoffed at the idea, preferring the weekly payment plan arrangements offered through dealers, wherein buyers made $5–$10 payments to the dealer every week to fully pay for their vehicle purchase.

The idea of financing vehicles wasn't entirely new. Finance plans for organs and sewing machines predate the first automobile finance deal. But historians credit the rise of automobile financing as cementing the idea that Americans could buy big-ticket items through loan, interest, and payment arrangements.

The earliest auto finance deals included a sizable down payment and a one-year payoff term. Nearly a hundred years later, the average loan term is nearly six years, and, depending on a buyer's credit, the total cost of interest for these loans may well exceed the value of the vehicle purchased.

In short, you could make the case that, without the variety of financing and lease options available to would-be vehicle owners, the cost of purchasing a vehicle would likely be out of reach for many American households.

The situation begs a key question: Why are Americans so determined to own their own vehicles? The easy answer is that we live in a car-focused culture, where owning a car is tantamount to an inalienable right of citizens.

Indeed, in the 1920s, as automobile financing began to gain a full head of steam, federal regulators cautioned banks about the rightness and risk of financing cars, given the household debt these arrangements created for many American families.

The regulators backed down in the face of pushback from newspaper editorial writers, and even the banks themselves, who essentially made the case that it's the right of every American to own their own vehicle. Transportation had become a necessary part of life, and vehicle ownership helped the masses get where they needed to go.

In more recent years, however, the idea of owning a car has lost some of its luster.

There seem to be two key reasons for this shift in attitude—the inflow of people back to urban areas, where mass transportation systems can make the necessity of buying a vehicle seem less critical, and the continued rising costs of owning a vehicle.

I've had dozens of conversations with dealers and friends about the seeming lack of interest our children show toward getting a driver's license and owning their own vehicle. For many of us, it's a head-scratcher. We've been brought up to believe that if you didn't own your own car, you were missing out on something.

But the younger generation sees it differently. Many don't have the high-paying jobs they expected when they left college. Many still have significant debt on their hands. Many still live with their parents, where the existence of one or two cars lessens their need to own a vehicle for themselves.

It's out of this backdrop that ride-sharing services have emerged. They offer a convenient, low out-of-pocket cost alternative to owning a car.

To date, the advent of ride-sharing services hasn't been terribly disruptive for dealers. We continue to sell record numbers of new and used vehicles, even as ride-sharing services gain in popularity. These services have caused significant consternation and some disruption for long-established transportation providers, like rental car and taxi companies.

If dealers only had to worry about ride-sharing services, I wouldn't be terribly concerned about their future prosperity and relevance as retailers. But when you view this trend in conjunction with the rise of self-driving cars, I see a significant problem for dealers and dealerships as we know them today.

WHY RIDE-SHARING AND SELF-DRIVING CARS COULD DISRUPT DEALERS

I think it's fair to say that only a minority of vehicle buyers today fully understand the total cost of owning a vehicle.

Beyond the purchase price and finance terms, vehicle owners pay for gas, fees for license and registration, insurance, maintenance, and parking and tolls, among other expenses. It's not uncommon for all of these associated costs to equal or surpass the monthly finance or lease payment vehicle buyers consider in the cost of owning a vehicle.

But an even smaller number of vehicle owners understand the inefficiency of their investment in a car.

I recently read a study that suggests that, for most Americans, their vehicles sit idle more than 90 percent of the time. Think about it: Your car isn't running while you sleep, spend time with family (unless it's in the car on a trip), or work at home or the office.

Some might believe that the advent of self-driving car technology is the product of tech-heads who have nothing better to do than come up with new innovations that solve a problem—people driving cars—that doesn't really exist.

But I think the tech-heads are on to something, particularly when you consider their efforts to develop self-driving cars as an attack on the inherent inefficiency of vehicles on the ground today and the investment their owners have made in them.

Self-driving cars appear to solve these problems. They show up at your door when you need them to take you to work or the grocery store. They drop you off and leave to serve someone else. They are always on the go, moving from one place to the other. Ostensibly, the only downtime for these vehicles would be the time required for fueling, maintenance, and upkeep—something the tech-heads are likely trying to address.

On the surface, self-driving vehicles would not appear to pose a lot of disruption and risk for dealers. You could make the case that someone will have to sell these vehicles to consumers and service the cars when they need it.

But I think this analysis misses three critical realities—that cars are increasingly unaffordable, save for the financing arrangements that make vehicle ownership feasible; that the next generation of buyers isn't as keen on owning a vehicle compared to prior generations; and that a self-driving car in every driveway defeats the investment and operational efficiencies these vehicles are intended to deliver.

When viewed through this lens, I start to see trouble for dealers.

It would seem to be a natural progression of the market for large, fleet-like organizations to actually own the self-driving vehicles, providing them to consumers on a pay-as-you go basis. Likewise, these organizations would have the sufficient scale and size to maintain their fleets of self-driving cars. It doesn't seem feasible that these companies would want to send their cars to a disparate network of dealerships for service, rather than have them show up at a centralized facility when it's time to change the oil, detail the car, or recharge a power source.

Perhaps the good news is that these tectonic shifts in the current landscape of vehicle ownership and driving habits will require a significant amount of time before they pose any serious risk to dealers.

But that's exactly why I fear dealers and the entire automotive retail industry may well be approaching a "Kodak moment."

Many readers may be aware that the Eastman Kodak Company is known as a poster child for a colossal, costly strategic error.

The company invented digital photography in 1975, decades before digital cameras and smartphones became the picture-taking norm for most American families.

But, according to published articles, Kodak executives considered the technology as cute and inconsequential compared to its film-based business model, which had propelled it to become a household brand name and a successful market leader.

As the story goes, Kodak wasn't unaware of the threats to its business. It knew digital photography was gaining ground. But the company reportedly took comfort in research that suggested it had ten years before this nascent technology would pose any kind of significant threat.

The end result wasn't pretty. Kodak filed for bankruptcy protection in 2012, laying off a reported 3,000-plus employees. Today, Kodak is profitable as an imaging technology company, but it is hardly the dominant brand it used to be.

And therein lies a lesson for dealers that's worth remembering: While it's difficult to know how the convergence of ride-sharing and self-driving vehicles will play out, a change in the nature of vehicle ownership, and the role dealers play in facilitating vehicle purchases, may well happen faster than any of us think. To me, the future seems less about selling and servicing cars and more about transportation.

As these trends unfold, perhaps this quote from Mark Twain will help us all remain vigilant and on-point: "It ain't what you don't know that gets you into trouble. It's what you know for sure that just ain't so."

15

FARMER TODD FINDS HIS BLUE OCEAN

A few years ago, I was a family farmer.

I didn't earn this descriptor because my family and I were out working corn and soybean fields, or raising livestock, in northwest Illinois.

My stint as a family farmer came about because I had purchased a farm property near Galena, Illinois, to serve as a family getaway and vacation spot.

The property included a farmhouse, some outbuildings, and about a hundred acres of tillable land. As the owner, I legally became a farmer, one of a growing number of farm owners for whom farming isn't a primary occupation.

Not long after I bought the place, I got a call from Todd.

A few years earlier, he'd rented my farmland from the prior owner. He'd heard I might be interested in leasing the property.

I did my homework, and we worked out a deal. The next spring, my family and I heard and saw Todd quite a bit as he prepared and planted the ground.

Over time, we became friends. He even let me drive his tractor a time or two without keeping his hand on the throttle lever.

I've been thinking a lot about Todd as I consider the future of the retail automotive industry. Believe it or not, his family's story has a few uncanny parallels with today's car business. And the way he's adapted to a dramatically changed business seems instructive to share here.

A BLUE OCEAN ON THE ILLINOIS PRAIRIE

About a decade ago, I ran across the book *Blue Ocean Strategy: How to Create Uncontested Market Space and Make the Competition Irrelevant*, by W. Chan Kim and Renée Mauborgne. At the most basic level, the book is about finding a differentiator, or niche, within your market that you can call your own.

I read the book in the early days of vAuto, when our solution wasn't quite ready or right to serve the needs of dealers.

The "blue ocean" for vAuto proved to be a blend of cutting-edge market data and metrics, the Velocity Method of Management, and dedicated performance managers committed to each client dealer's success.

This strategic recipe proved to be a game-changer, and, despite competitors, vAuto went on to pioneer a new category of dealership software.

I doubt my farmer friend Todd has read *Blue Ocean Strategy*. But he'd make a great case study, given the way he's transformed and transitioned his business to meet the realities of a vastly different marketplace.

Some background on Todd: He's a third-generation farmer. He grew up in the same house he lives in today. At various times, the family farm operation raised dairy cows, chickens, pigs, corn, soybeans, sugar beets, and wheat. Over the years, the farm grew in size, with Todd's family owning a little less than four hundred acres.

Enter the recession of the 1980s. Farmers faced high interest rates, market price controls, and ever-higher costs for equipment, feed, seed, fertilizer, and other essentials to modern-day farm operations. Foreclosures were rampant. The weather wasn't all that great either, and Todd's family faced several lean years.

Todd's father had taught him well, though. Thanks to their willingness to diversify their operations, and their scrappy nature, the family wasn't among the thousands of farmers across America who sold their stakes, unable to meet their financial obligations and compete with ever-smaller returns on their investments and increased risks. Many sold their operations for a song to increasingly corporate-owned buyers.

Todd saw the writing on the wall. He knew he'd need to become more efficient and penny-wise if he intended to keep the farm and provide a viable future for his children. He understood that he needed to do three things at once—get more land, specialize his crop selections, and wring every ounce of additional expense and inefficiency out of his operation.

"We made a conscious decision to understand where the other guys were going and find a way to go somewhere else," he says. The strategy resulted in a patchwork of leased properties, including mine. This quilt of land gave Todd sufficient options and scale to put his strategy into practice.

Todd understood his disadvantages as a smaller player in a business that seemed to increasingly tilt toward the advantage of bigger operators. I remember asking Todd how to tell the difference between a true-blue family farmer and a corporate-owned operation.

"Just look at the equipment," he told me. "Everything they run is bigger and better. It takes me about half a day to plant one hundred acres; they can do the same work in an hour."

I hadn't talked to Todd in several years because my family sold our farm. Thinking about him for this chapter prompted me to check in.

He and his family are doing great. They have added organic fruits and vegetables to their farm production list. He's seeing returns from the Christmas trees he planted a few years ago.

"I don't have any complaints, Dale," Todd told me. "I've managed to stay in business and provide a good future for my family. I don't know what tomorrow will bring. But as long as I don't take anything for granted, and keep looking for the next opportunity, we'll be fine."

Given the way the car business is going, Todd's words of wisdom are worth remembering, particularly for dealers who have yet to define their own blue ocean.

Epilogue

A LIFE LESSON FROM POPE FRANCIS

You don't meet many people who, in an instant, change your life.

I felt this way after I met with Pope Francis at the Vatican in early 2017.

The meeting was part of an organized trip to Rome, where our delegation met with church and government leaders. We were part of a nonprofit advocacy group, traveling to represent democratic ideals and protect civil rights. Nancy and I have been long-time supporters of the group, and the trip offered a once-in-a-lifetime opportunity we decided we had to take.

Our papal visit offered brief, one-on-one meetings with Pope Francis. In advance, I was pretty excited and very nervous.

I was also worried. Worried about what I would say. Then, I worried what I might not say. Then, I worried I might not know what to say or that I'd say the wrong thing.

You get the picture. As it turned out, I was pretty steady on my feet and in voice. We held hands, and I told His Holiness:

"Your Holy Father, my name is Dale, and I am from America. I would like to ask for your prayer and holy voice to speak out against hatred and the speech of hatred that is so prevalent in our country today."

Suddenly, I felt Pope Francis hold my arm and lean his head into my chest. I was confused. I didn't know what was happening. Then it hit me: Pope Francis is not just saying a prayer for me; he's saying a prayer *into* me, directed straight at my heart.

I've been around church leaders for a long time. I've asked rabbis and ministers to say a prayer when personal or family circumstances warranted the request.

But I have never, ever, felt what it's like when someone else actually takes my request to heart, says a prayer on my behalf, and delivers it directly into me.

Peace. Empowerment. Hope. Humility. Strength. Wonder. Those are the feelings and words that came to mind in the moment and later that day.

And I've been feeling, and thinking about, these same things ever since.

I now realize my meeting with Pope Francis was somewhat unique. At least, that's what the others in our group thought. They asked, "What'd you say?" and "Was he really holding you?"

Of course, I've spent a fair amount of time trying to figure out what I was supposed to learn, or take away, from the meeting. What, exactly, gave meaning to this moment, beyond the fact that I was meeting with the Pope?

After much thought, I've landed on two reasons why I found this meeting to be a life-changing moment:

I needed the life lesson. I've always considered myself to be a fair, decent person. But Pope Francis reminded me that I could be better. If the most respected and revered religious figure on earth can give his heart to me, a complete stranger, for a greater good, what can I do?

I've realized that the answer is pretty simple: It's to recognize and embrace the reality that every engagement or interaction with another person is an opportunity to have a positive impact.

The life lesson is relevant for everyone in retail automotive. My papal visit occurred in the homestretch of writing this book. Things happen for, and when, they do for a reason. I realize that while this book discusses a lot of obstacles and opportunities in retail automotive, it doesn't directly deal with matters of the heart and soul.

But more and more, I've come to realize that heart and soul is increasingly the essence of success in business, and especially the car business. The best, biggest, and brightest success will go to those among us who recognize and embrace that each customer engagement and interaction is either an opportunity to make a positive impact and create a bond, or it's a catalyst for the competition.

Perhaps the most fascinating aspect of the life lesson I drew from meeting Pope Francis is that I truly don't believe he was trying to teach me anything.

He was just doing what great individuals, and great leaders, do.

He was setting a good example, leaving it up to me, and you, to make of it as we will.

ABOUT THE AUTHOR

DALE POLLAK'S career in the automotive industry spans nearly four decades. As a dealer, technology entrepreneur, and best-selling author, Pollak has helped many successful automotive dealers in North America make dramatic improvements in their new and used vehicle operations.

Pollak pioneered the Velocity Method of Management™, an operational strategy that relies on live market data and insights to maximize a dealer's profitability and return on investment from their new and used vehicle inventories. Pollak crafted this approach during his years as a Cadillac dealer in Chicago in light of his unique circumstances of not being able to physically observe his used vehicle inventory.

This Velocity vision served as the foundation for vAuto, Incorporated, the company that Pollak founded in 2005. Since then, the company's technology and tools have been adopted by more than ten thousand dealerships in North America. In late 2010, Cox Automotive acquired vAuto. Pollak continues to guide strategic product development and integration for vAuto and other Cox Automotive companies. Prior to vAuto, Pollak helped build and lead Digital Motorworks, Incorporated to its successful acquisition in 2002.

Pollak has written three books that detail the application of the Velocity Method of Management™ in dealerships. The latest, *Velocity Overdrive: The Road to Reinvention*, was released in 2012.

Pollak holds a bachelor of science degree in business administration from Indiana University, a law degree from DePaul University's College of Law, and is a four-time winner of the American Jurisprudence Award. In addition, Pollak received the 2010 Ernst and Young Entrepreneur of the Year Award, and in 2011, Pollak was inducted into the Chicago Area Entrepreneurship Hall of Fame. In 2014, Pollak was named as Poling Chair at Indiana University's Kelley School of Business.